# Learning to Learn English
Learner's Book

# Learning to Learn English

A course in learner training

## Learner's Book

*Gail Ellis and
Barbara Sinclair*

CAMBRIDGE
UNIVERSITY PRESS

*To Norman Whitney with thanks*

Published by the Press Syndicate of the University of Cambridge
The Pitt Building, Trumpington Street, Cambridge CB2 1RP
40 West 20th Street, New York, NY 10011–4211, USA
10 Stamford Road, Oakleigh, Melbourne 3166, Australia

© Cambridge University Press 1989

First published 1989
Third printing 1993

Printed in Great Britain
by Scotprint Ltd, Musselburgh, Scotland

ISBN 0 521 33816 6 Learner's Book
ISBN 0 521 33817 4 Teacher's Book
ISBN 0 521 32876 4 Cassette

WV

# Contents

# Acknowledgements

We would like to thank the following people for their patience, support and encouragement: the Ellis family, Philip W. Sinclair, David Wharry and Helen Woodeson.

We are also grateful to the following:
Colleagues and pupils in France and at the British Council, Paris, 1983–7; colleagues and learners at the British Council, Munich, 1983–7 for providing valuable feedback; Peter Donovan and our editors Alison Baxter and Angela Wilde at Cambridge University Press for their interest, support and constructive advice; Roland Hindmarsh for providing the initial motivation; all those who gave us permission to record them and to use their photographs, examples of handwriting and points of view about language learning, and particularly Kate Pearce for her help; in addition, our thanks for all the guidance received from other sources.

We would like to thank the following people and institutions for piloting learner training materials and providing us with valuable feedback:
Institut für Sprachwissenschaft, Universität Bern, Switzerland; The Bell School, Cambridge; Eurocentre, Cambridge; The Newnham Language Centre, Cambridge; Ecole des Cadres, Courbevoie, France; Infop, Dijon-Longvic, France; Exeter College, Exeter; Institute for English Language, University of Lancaster; Instituto de Idiomas, Lima, Peru; International House, London; Formation Continue, Université Lumière Lyon 2, Lyon, France; British Council, Madrid; AMES, Melbourne, Australia; RMIT, Melbourne, Australia; Godmer House, Oxford; Formatique Développement, Paris, France; Institut Universitaire de Technologie, Paris, France; Institut Catholique de Paris, Paris, France; AMES, Perth, Australia; FAO; Rome, Italy; Cambridge Centre for Languages, Sawston; Centre de Formation de Formateurs, Université des Sciences Humaines, Strasbourg, France; Stanton School of English, Tokyo, Japan; CAVILAM, Vichy, France; ENAC, Toulouse, France; Dr Anna Chamot; Liz Hamp-Lyons; Dr J. Michael O'Malley; Lorna Rowsell; Joan Rubin; Stephen Slater.

The authors and publishers are grateful to the following for permission to reproduce copyright material:
*New Scientist* (article on p.15); S. A. Spa Monopole (advertisement on p.15); *The Guardian* (articles on p.15 by Jane Cameron, Victoria Macdonald and London Weather Centre and masthead on p.41); Tony Buzan (graphs on p.17 and extract on p.82 adapted from *Use Your Head* by Tony Buzan, Ariel Books and BBC Publications); Dr D. G. Hessayon (extract from *The House Plant Expert* by Dr D. G. Hessayon, PBI Publications); Brooke Bond Oxo Limited (PG Tips and Oxo flats on p.41); BBC External

# Acknowledgements

Services (World Service logo on p.41); London Underground Limited (logo and ticket on p.41); Kellogg's Corn Flakes (on p.41) reproduced by kind permission of Kellogg Company; stamps (on p.41) reproduced by permission of Royal Mail Letters – a division of the Post Office; Cadbury Limited (logo on p.41); Barnaby's Picture Library (photographs on p.57); *What's on in London* (information on p.58); Brown's Restaurants, Cambridge, Oxford and Brighton (menu on p.83); *Woman's Weekly* (extract on p.89 from "Surgeon on Call" by Janet Ferguson); Longman Group UK Limited (adapted extracts on p.90 from *Panorama* by Ray Williams); The Provost and Scholars of King's College, Cambridge (photograph on p.102 of *Sanditon* by Jane Austen); W. & R. Chambers Limited (extract on p.12 from *Chambers Universal Learners' Dictionary*); W. Collins, Son & Company Limited (extract on p.12 from *Collins 'Gem' French-English, English-French Dictionary*).

Illustrations by Jerry Collins (pp.22, 58), Clyde Pearson (pp.37, 57) and Shaun Williams (p.38). Text artwork by Wenham Arts and Ace Art.
Book designed by Peter Ducker MSTD.

# Introduction

*Learning to Learn English* aims to help you:
— become a more effective learner of English
— take on more responsibility for your own learning
by helping you to consider factors which may affect your language learning and to discover the learning strategies that suit you best. This is what we call *learner training*.

This book will be used during your course together with your course book or other materials. Your teacher will guide you.

You will find questions to discuss, activities and suggestions to help you with your language learning. In class you will be asked to discuss your ideas about language learning with other students so that you can learn from each other.

Your Learner's Book has two stages of training (see the diagram on page 2):

Stage 1 Preparation for language learning

Stage 2 Skills training

These two stages aim to take you step by step to the point where you can plan your own study programme for learning English independently, if you wish.

You will find the following symbols used in this book:

 = pair work

 = group work

 = class discussion with teacher

 = recorded on the cassette

# Framework for Learner Training

Keep a record of the learner training you have covered by ticking the boxes (✓) as you finish each section.

| Stage 1  Preparation for language learning | |
|---|---|
| 1.1  What do you expect from your course? | |
| 1.2  What sort of language learner are you? | |
| 1.3  Why do you need or want to learn English? | |
| 1.4  How do you organise your learning? | |
| 1.5  How motivated are you? | |
| 1.6  What can you do in a self-access centre? | |

| Stage 2  Skills training | How do you feel . . .? | What do you know . . .? | How well are you doing? | What do you need to do next? | How do you prefer to learn/practise . . .? | Do you need to build up your confidence? | How do you organise . . .? |
|---|---|---|---|---|---|---|---|
| *Skills* | Step 1 | Step 2 | Step 3 | Step 4 | Step 5 | Step 6 | Step 7 |
| 2.1  Extending vocabulary | | | | | | | |
| 2.2  Dealing with grammar | | | | | | | |
| 2.3  Listening | | | | | | | |
| 2.4  Speaking | | | | | | | |
| 2.5  Reading | | | | | | | |
| 2.6  Writing | | | | | | | |

# Stage 1
## Preparation for language learning

# 1.1 What do you expect from your course?

  1. Ask and answer the following questions.

    a) Do you think you are good at learning languages? Why or why not?
    b) What do you think is the best way to learn a new language? Why?
    c) What kinds of activities do you think should be included in your course? Why?

 2. Discuss your ideas with the rest of your class.

# 1.2 What sort of language learner are you?

Try the following quiz. Tick (✓) your answers to the questions.

| | Usually | Sometimes | (Almost) never | Don't know |
|---|---|---|---|---|
| 1. Did/do you get good results in grammar tests? | | | | |
| 2. Do you have a good memory for new words? | | | | |
| 3. Do you hate making mistakes? | | | | |
| 4. In class, do you get irritated if mistakes are not corrected? | | | | |
| 5. Is your pronunciation better when you read aloud than when you have a conversation? | | | | |
| 6. Do you wish you had more time to think before speaking? | | | | |
| 7. Did/do you enjoy being in a class? | | | | |
| 8. Do you find it difficult to pick up more than two or three words of a new language when you are on holiday abroad? | | | | |
| 9. Do you like to learn new grammar rules, words, etc. by heart? | | | | |

## 1.2 What sort of language learner are you?

How to calculate your score:

Score: 3 points for each *Usually*
      2 points for each *Sometimes*
      1 point for each *Almost never* or *never*
      0 points for each *Don't know*

Total score: ☐

Now read the appropriate comments on pages 8–9.

## Score: 23-27 points Analytic?

You may feel it is very important to be as accurate as possible all the time. You probably prefer the sort of language learning where you need to think carefully: for example, when you are doing grammar exercises, working out the meanings of words, practising pronunciation, etc. This is very often the sort of language learning you do in class or when you are studying alone.

You may be able to improve your language learning. Look at the following suggestions.

## Score: 14-22 A mixture?

You may find that you do not fall exactly into either of the categories marked *Analytic?* or *Relaxed?*. Many people are a mixture and learn in different ways at different times depending on the situation and what they are doing.

### Suggestion

Look at the descriptions for *Analytic?* and *Relaxed?*. You may find that you are more similar to one than the other and this could help you to think about what areas of your learning you might improve. If you can't decide now, try to do this during your course.

## Suggestions

You could improve your fluency by:
- *trying to speak more*
  For example, try talking to English-speaking friends, tourists, etc. as often as possible.
- *not worrying too much about your mistakes*
  Trying to be correct all the time is hard work and can stop you from communicating well. Although making mistakes is an important part of the learning process, don't always try to correct yourself immediately. Remember that the people you speak to won't be listening for your mistakes, but for what you are trying to say. After you have finished speaking, you can usually remember the mistakes you want to work on; this is a good time to make a note to yourself to do something about them.
- *depending on yourself*
  Outside the classroom you won't always have a dictionary or a teacher to help you, so don't be afraid to depend on yourself: you probably know more than you think.

## Score: 0-8 points Not sure?

Your score does not mean that you are not a good language learner. Perhaps this is the first time you have thought about the way you learn. To know more about this can be very useful in helping you to become a more effective language learner.

### Suggestion

You can find out some general information about learning languages by looking at the descriptions marked *Analytic?* and *Relaxed?*. During your course, try to become more aware of the ways you learn. This can help you decide which areas of your learning you might improve.

**Score: 9-13 points   Relaxed?**

You seem to 'pick up' languages without really making too much effort and you usually enjoy communicating with people. You may sometimes feel, however, that you should be learning more grammar rules, but you probably don't enjoy this and quickly lose interest.

You may be able to improve your language learning. Look at the following suggestions.

*Suggestions*

- *try finding more time to learn*
  You may need to spend more time thinking about and practising things like grammar, pronunciation, etc. Try to organise a regular time for learning.
- *try being more self-critical*
  You probably need to correct yourself more. You may not worry or even notice when you make mistakes, but if you try to become more aware of the mistakes you make regularly, you may find it easier to do something about them.

*Note*: You may like to try this quiz again after you have done some more learning, to compare the results.

# 1.3 Why do you need or want to learn English?

 **1 Analysing your needs**

Before you start your course, it is a good idea to think carefully about what you need or want English for. You could analyse your needs like this.

a) Decide on your *main purpose* for learning English e.g. for work.
b) Make a list of the *specific situations* where you need to use English e.g. speaking on the telephone, answering enquiries, giving information, writing business letters.
c) Decide which *skills* you need for each situation: extending vocabulary, dealing with grammar, listening, speaking, reading or writing.

You should then have a better idea about which skills you need to work on and be able to establish your priorities.

Here is an example of how one learner analysed his needs. Stig is a Swedish Youth Hostel warden who needs English for his work. He filled in the following chart. You will find a blank chart on page 109 in the Appendix, which you could use to analyse your own needs.

| Situations | Skills | | | | | |
|---|---|---|---|---|---|---|
| | Vocabulary (✓) | Grammar (✓) | Listening (✓) | Speaking (✓) | Reading (✓) | Writing (✓) |
| Youth Hostel Reception Desk | | | | | | |
| – welcoming new guests | ✓ | | | ✓ | | |
| – giving YH information | ✓ | | | ✓ | | |
| – explaining regulations | ✓ | ✓ | | ✓ | | |
| – answering enquiries | ✓ | | ✓ | ✓ | | |
| – putting up notices | ✓ | ✓ | | | | ✓ |

## 2   Prioritising your needs

*How much do you know / can you do already?*

Stig used an assessment scale from 1 to 5:
1 = this is the standard I would like to reach – my goal.
5 = I can do very little. I am a long way from my goal.
He considered each skill that he needed and circled the number that he felt represented his position on the scale, as follows:

| Extending vocabulary | Dealing with grammar | Listening | Speaking | Reading | Writing |
|---|---|---|---|---|---|
| 1 | 1 | 1 | 1 | ①| 1 |
| 2 | 2 | 2 | ② | 2 | 2 |
| 3 | ③ | ③ | 3 | 3 | 3 |
| ④ | 4 | 4 | 4 | 4 | ④ |
| 5 | 5 | 5 | 5 | 5 | 5 |

He was then able to see more clearly what he needed to improve most.

You will find a blank self-assessment scale in the Appendix (page 110) for your own use.

*What are your priorities?*

Stig then gave each skill a priority rating from 1 to 6:
1 = highest priority
6 = lowest priority

*I thought I needed to improve my speaking, but now I realise that it is mainly vocabulary that is missing. My speaking is quite good, in fact. I also realise that I need to concentrate on my listening and writing. I can read English quite well – I don't need to do it much, anyway.*

Stig, Sweden

| Skill | Priority rating |
|---|---|
| Extending vocabulary | 1 |
| Dealing with grammar | 4 |
| Listening | 2 |
| Speaking | 5 |
| Reading | 6 |
| Writing | 3 |

You could prioritise your own needs in the same way. If you do this, it will give you a clearer idea about which sections in Stage 2 of this book would be most useful for you. It will also give you a basis for negotiating the content of your course with the other members of your class and your teacher. You will find a blank record of priorities in the Appendix (page 110).

# 1.4 How do you organise your learning?

## 1 Have you got a dictionary?

You could use a chart like the one below to make a survey of dictionaries and to help you choose one for your own use.

| Title | Date published | Number of headwords | Bilingual/ Monolingual | Portable? | Examples of how words are used? |
|---|---|---|---|---|---|
| *Chambers Universal Learners' Dictionary* | *1980* | *45,000* | *Monolingual* | *Yes* | *Yes* |
| *Collins French-English English-French Dictionary* | *1988* | *over 40,000* | *Bilingual* | *Very* | *No* |

*Suggestion:* When assessing a dictionary for your own use, think of a word you already know and look it up.
 – Can you find it easily?
 – Do you understand the definition?
 – Does it give clear examples of how the word is used?
 – Does it give a phonetic transcription?

**prospect**
**public prosecutor** *nc* a lawyer who prosecutes on behalf of the state.
**prospect** [(*Brit and Amer*) 'prospekt] *ncu* **1** an outlook for the future; a view of what one may expect to happen: *He didn't like the prospect of going abroad; He has a job with good prospects.* **2** (*formal*) a view or scene: *a prospect of trees and fields.* – [prə'spekt, (*Amer*) 'prospekt] *vi* to make a search, *eg* for gold or other minerals: *He is prospecting for gold.*
**prospective** [(*Brit and Amer*) prə'spektiv] *adj* (*attrib*) likely or expected; future: *They want to sell their house, and already have a prospective buyer; He is the prospective Liberal candidate for this district.* – *(Amer)* 'prospektər] *nc a*

*protégé of the Prime Mini*
**protein** ['prouti:n] *ncu* (*te* of substances present which are necessary as beings and animals: *O Eat plenty of protein!*
**pro tem** [prou'tem] [prou'tempəri]) (*fon* time being: *He is pres*
**protest** [prə'test] **1** *vi t* *They are protesting a* *vt* (*esp formal or lite* *esp against oppositi* *meant no harm;* ['proutest] *nc a st* tion of objection ...*test. (attrib) a*

**propriety**

**propriety** [prə'praiiti] *n* (*seemliness*) bienséance *f*, convenance *f*.
**prose** [prouz] *n* prose *f*; (*SCOL: translation*) thème *m*.
**prosecute** ['prosikju:t] *vt* poursuivre; **prosecution** [-'kju:ʃən] *n* poursuites *fpl* judiciaires; (*accusing side*) accusation *f*; **prosecutor** *n* procureur *m*; (*also*: **public prosecutor**) ministère public.
**prospect** *n* ['prospekt] perspective *f*; (*hope*) espoir *m*, chances *fpl* // *vt, vi* [prə'spekt] prospecter; ~**s** *npl* (*for work etc*) possibilités *fpl* d'avenir, débouchés *mpl*; **prospective** [-'spektiv] *a* (*possible*) éventuel(le); (*future*) futur(e).
**prospectus** [prə'spektəs] *n* prospectus *m*.
**prosperity** [prə'speriti] *n* prospérité *f*.
**prostitute** ['prostitju:t] *n* prostituée *f*.
**protect** [prə'tekt] *vt* protéger; ~**ion** *n* protection *f*; ~**ive** *a* protecteur(trice).
**protein** ['prouti:n] *n* protéine *f*.
**protest** *n* ['proutest] protestation *f* // *vb* [prə'test] *vi* protester // *vt* protester de.
**Protestant** ['protistənt] *a, n* protestant(e).
**protester** [prə'testə*] *n* manifesta...

**205**

**providing** [prə'vaidiŋ] *cj* à condition que + *sub*.
**province** ['provins] *n* province *f*; **provincial** [prə'vinʃəl] *a* provincial(e).
**provision** [prə'viʒən] *n* (*supply*) provision *f*; (*supplying*) fourniture *f*; approvisionnement *m*; (*stipulation*) disposition *f*; ~**s** *npl* (*food*) provisions *fpl*; ~**al** *a* provisoire.
**proviso** [prə'vaizəu] *n* condition *f*.
**provocative** [prə'vokativ] *a* provocateur(trice), provocant(e).
**provoke** [prə'vəuk] *vt* provoquer; inciter.
**prow** [prau] *n* proue *f*.
**prowess** ['prauis] *n* prouesse *f*.
**prowl** [praul] *vi* (*also*: ~ **about**, ~ **around**) rôder // *n*: **on the ~** à l'affût; ~**er** *n* rôdeur/euse.
**proxy** ['proksi] *n* procuration *f*.
**prudent** ['pru:dnt] *a* prudent(e).
**prudish** ['pru:diʃ] *a* prude, pudibond(e).
**prune** [pru:n] *n* pruneau *m* // *vt* élaguer.
**pry** [prai] *vi*: **to ~ into** fourrer son nez dans.
**PS** *n abbr* (= *postscript*) p.s.
**psalm** [sa:m] *n* psaume *m*.
**pseudo-** ['sju:dəu] *prefix* pseudo-:
**pseudonym** *n* ...

**P.T.O.**

## 2   Have you got a grammar book?

You could use a chart like the one below to help you choose a grammar book for your own use.

| Title | Date published | Bilingual/ Monolingual | Clear index? | Easy to understand? | Examples in context? | Exercises? | Answers to exercises? |
|---|---|---|---|---|---|---|---|
| *A Very Simple Grammar of English, LTP* | *1985* | *Monolingual* | *Yes* | *Yes* | *Yes* | *No* | *No* |
| *English Grammar In Use, CUP* | *1985* | *Monolingual* | *Yes* | *Yes* | *Yes* | *Yes* | *Yes* |

*Suggestion:* When assessing a grammar book you might like to use, think of a grammatical point that you already know well, for example 'some and any'.
– Can you find it easily?
– Do you understand the explanation in the book?
– Does the book tell you enough?

## 3   What other resources have you got?

How many of the following resources can you use, either in your school or outside? Tick (✓) the ones that are available to you.

☐ self-access centre

☐ language laboratory

☐ video recorder/player

☐ video camera

☐ computer

☐ library

☐ English language radio programmes

☐ English language TV programmes/films

☐ English language films at the cinema

☐ shops for English language newspapers, magazines, books, videos, records, cassettes, etc.

☐ English language clubs for conversation, etc.

## 1.4   How do you organise your learning?

Why not find out more about the resources you are interested in? You could keep records like this:

a)   *Radio*

| Radio stations | Frequencies | Interesting programmes | Day | Time |
|---|---|---|---|---|
| *BBC World Service (Italy)* | *15070 kHz or 12095 kHz* | *World News News about Britain* | *Saturdays* | *11 a.m. GMT 11.09 a.m. GMT* |

b)   *Television*

| TV Channel | Interesting programmes, films | Day | Time |
|---|---|---|---|
| *A2 (France)* | *Les Enfants du Rock (interviews with pop stars, often in English)* | *Saturdays* | *23.20* |

c)   *Cinema*

| Name of Cinema | Where | Interesting films | Day | Time |
|---|---|---|---|---|
| *Forum Orient Express* | *Forum des Halles, Paris* | *Hairspray* | *Monday 27 June* | *21.35* |

d)   *Shops*

| Name of Shop | Where | Items | Cost | Other details |
|---|---|---|---|---|
| *Words' Worth* | *Schellingstrasse, Munich 40* | *English books, paperbacks, magazines* | *DM 20 per paperback (approx.)* | *Can order books, very helpful staff.* |

e)   *English clubs*

| Name | Where | Activities | When |
|---|---|---|---|
| *Link-up* | *San Gervasio de Casolas 107, Barcelona* | *English meals and conversation video nights, excursions, music, poetry, reading, etc.* | *Thursdays, Fridays, Saturdays, 7.30 – midnight* |

14

## 4   How do you organise your materials?

Have you considered the following suggestions?

*Personal libraries for listening, viewing, reading, etc.*

If you wish to create your own library, you could keep your materials:
– alphabetically by title
– alphabetically by name of speaker/author
– by topic
– by degree of difficulty, for example E = easy, OK = right level, D = difficult
Can you add any more ideas?
   It is a good idea to *label* your materials clearly and to include information such as:
– title of newspaper
– date produced or collected
– where collected

*Personal language banks*

For information about these, see Step 5 in the following sections of this book:
2.1  Extending vocabulary
2.2  Dealing with grammar
2.6  Writing

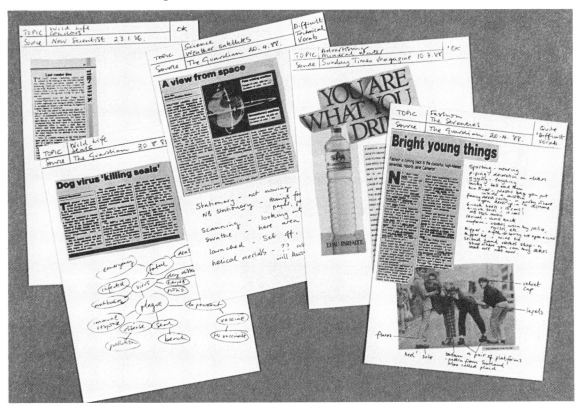

## 5 How much time have you got to learn English?

Even if you can only manage to learn for ten minutes a week, you will still be able to make progress if you organise your time efficiently.

Try to calculate the approximate amount of time you spend doing the following things in a typical week:

| Activity | Time (approx.) |
|---|---|
| Sleeping | |
| Getting up | |
| Preparing for and eating meals | |
| Short breaks (snacks, coffee, etc.) | |
| Your routine time in work / at school | |
| Travel to and from work/school | |
| Preparation for work/school at home | |
| Total time | |
| How much time does this give you for learning English in a typical week? | |

| | |
|---|---|
| Is the time available more or less than you expected? | More/Less |
| If less, are there any activities you could give up or spend less time doing? | Yes/No |

 How is the amount of time available to you going to affect your language learning? Are you being realistic about what you can achieve?

## 6 How do you organise your time?

No matter how organised your materials are, you need to organise your time efficiently for learning. For example, arranging regular times for reviewing your learning can help you to remember more.

The following graphs show you how you can improve your memory in this way. Figure 1 shows how it is possible to forget 80% of what you have learnt within 24 hours if you don't review.

Figure 2 shows how regular reviews can help you to keep your recall level high. Note how it is important to start your reviews just at the time when you feel you can remember the most, usually about ten minutes after learning.

Can you build regular review sessions into your language learning programme?

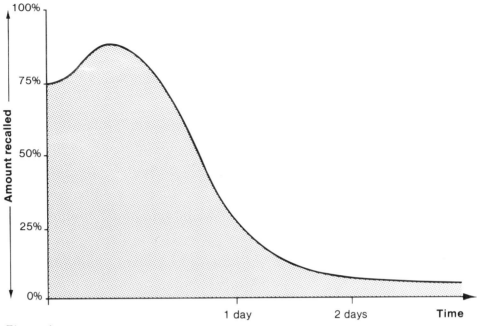

*Figure 1*

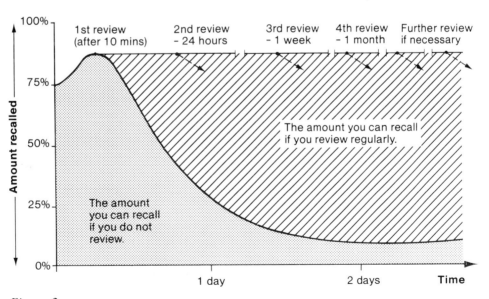

*Figure 2*

17

# 1.5  How motivated are you?

Your motivation can affect your progress.

a) Most learners go through various stages of motivation. It can be useful to keep a record of your high and low points and to analyse why you felt like that at the time. You could use a graph to keep a record of your motivation levels during your course. You will find one in the Appendix on page 113. Here is an example of a graph that an English learner used during one week of her French language course in France.

 b) Discuss the following questions in class.
   – How motivated do you feel now? Why?
   – How did you feel yesterday? Why?
   – What things might affect your motivation during your course?

## 1.5 How motivated are you?

Name: Geraldine                                    Date: 11 – 15.7.88

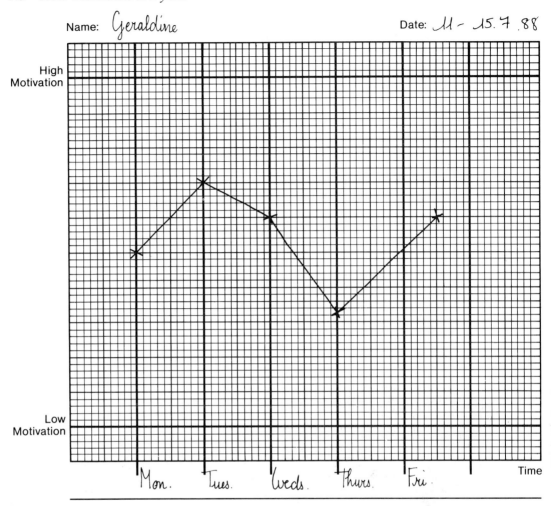

| Day | Comments |
|---|---|
| Mon. | Felt a bit nervous at first. It wasn't too hard, so I felt better at the end of the day. I like my teacher! |
| Tues. | Felt better. I sat next to Alfredo — he's very nice. The role play this afternoon was good fun! |
| Weds. | OK. Felt a bit tired at the end of the day. |
| Thurs. | Couldn't understand the grammar today. It was too hot in class. I got a headache. |
| Fri. | We were videoed today — it was great! Looking forward to our trip to Paris tomorrow. |

# 1.6 What can you do in a self-access centre*?

## 1 In class

 Discuss the following points.

a) What does *self-access learning* mean?
b) What do you already know about your school's self-access centre?
c) What do you think are the purposes of a self-access centre?
d) Have you already had some experience of a self-access centre? What were the advantages or disadvantages?
   If you have not yet had any experience of a self-access centre, what do you think the advantages and disadvantages would be?

*Your school may have a different name for it.

## 2 In the self-access centre

Try doing some research. Choose one of the following questions to investigate. Make brief notes so that you can tell the class what you have found.

a) What kinds of activities can you do in the centre? For example:
  − Can you work on your pronunciation?
  − Can you practise the present perfect?

b) What kinds of materials are available? For example:
  − newspapers
  − specially written exercises with answers
  − materials for beginners/intermediate/advanced levels

c) How can you find the materials you want to use? For example:
  − Are they colour coded?
  − Is there a catalogue?
  − Is there somebody to find them for you?

d) Can you get help when you are working? For example:
  − from a technician
  − from a librarian
  − from a teacher/helper

e) Does your school suggest a way of keeping a record of what you do there? If so, what is it?

Ask your teacher if you have any other questions about the self-access centre. How do you feel about working in the self-access centre now?

## 3 Time to experiment

If you have never worked in a self-access centre before, you may find it a little strange at first and you may spend a lot of time just looking around and thinking about what to do. Don't worry about this − you are not wasting your time, but learning to think critically about what might be useful and enjoyable for you in your learning.

You may begin to do something and then find that it is boring or too easy or too difficult. Perhaps you just don't feel like it. This is normal. Leave it and try something else. You may need to try several different things until you discover what is best for you.

Don't expect to be 'successful' every time. Even if you don't learn anything new about the language, you can learn something about yourself and the way you learn.

Try the following experiment. Use the self-access centre for 1–2 hours for some self-study. Afterwards, discuss your personal experiences and feelings with other learners.

You might like to consider the following points.

a) What were your aims before you started? Why?
b) What activities/materials did you choose? Why?
c) What were your strategies for using the materials?   ⟫→

d) Were your strategies useful/successful?
e) Did you have any problems? If so, what were they?
f) If you try self-access learning again, what do you think you will do/try next? Why?

How do you feel about self-access learning now?
Try repeating this experiment regularly.

## 4   One learner's experience

a) Read what Pierre says about his experiences in the self-access centre in his school. Can you predict how he finished his sentences (i)–(v)?
Listen to the cassette to check your predictions.

i) I always seem to have problems when I listen to English, so I decided to listen ................................................................................................. .

ii) When I got in there, I had a look at the cassettes and found one of the day before yesterday's news. I thought it wouldn't be too difficult because I had looked at a newspaper yesterday and we had discussed the news in class too. After a couple of minutes though, I got bored, so I decided to ................................................................................................. .

iii) First, I read the whole article as quickly as I could – just to get the main ideas. There were a lot of words to do with parts of the bicycle that I didn't know, so I decided to ........................................................................ .

iv) Generally, I think my strategy was good, but I found I didn't really need the list of words and their translations that I had made. I think a diagram of a bicycle with labels might ........................................................ .

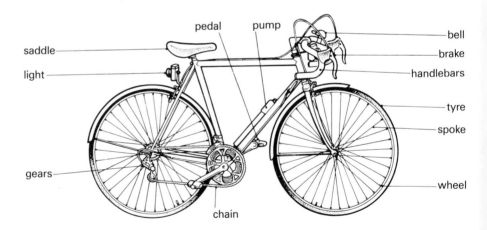

v) The only problem I had was that my friend kept trying to talk to me and I don't like ................................................................................................. .

vi) I enjoyed using the self-access centre, though it took a while for me to find something to do.

 b) How useful do you think Pierre's strategies were? Why? Would they be useful for you? Why or why not?

### 5 Keeping records

Can you think of any good reasons for keeping a record of what you have done during your self-access learning sessions? Make a list and discuss.

If you are interested in keeping records:

a) Decide *why* you want to keep a record and *how much detail* you want to record. Look at page 24 for some learners' ideas. Is there a method that would suit you? You can probably think of other ideas.

   Remember, if you are keeping a record, it is for *you* to look at and see your progress. It can be very motivating to look back after some time and see what you have done. It is also useful if you want to test yourself to see what you can remember, or if you want to repeat something. It is therefore important that your record really does help you to monitor your work and your progress.

b) When you have decided on your personal format, show it to somebody else for their comments. Try using it. You might decide to change your design.

>>>→

**SELF-ACCESS RECORD CARD**

Mª Dolores Ruíz Ruíg
Class: 2B
WHAT: "Clusters" by Colin Mortimer (CUP) Units 6/7/8
WHEN: 9/4
WHY: to practise pronunciation
HOW: listening + repeating + recording myself + listening
FOLLOW UP: "sp" "st" "sk" are hard! need more practice. Will try again next week

**NOVEMBER**

| | | | | |
|---|---|---|---|---|
| Monday | 3 | 10 | 17 | 24 |
| Tuesday | 4 | 11 | 18 | 25 |
| Wednesday | 5 | 12 | 19 | 26 |
| Thursday | 6 | 13 | 20 | 27 |
| Friday | 7 | 14 | 21 | 28 |
| Saturday | 1 | 8 | 15 | 22 | 29 |
| Sunday | 2 | 9 | 16 | 23 | 30 |

**Week 48** — 22 Saturday · 20 Thursday

Vocab  Reading  grammar

| Date | Exercise | Topic | Results | Comments |
|---|---|---|---|---|
| 2/5 | 10 b | present perfect | 90% | |
| 8/5 | 19 c | pres. perfect continuous | 50% | get help from teacher try again! |

**NOVEMBER SELF-ACCESS WEEK!**

Week 47 — 17 Monday · 18 Tuesday · 19 Wednesday

2.0 Read "Has the face of marriage changed?" New Society 18/3

Listened to recording of "Today" from Radio 4.

4.0 Wrote summary for class magazine.

Notes: Interesting!

Courtship
elopement
spouse

good part about nuclear energy
- meltdown point
- half-life
"what a load of poppycock" (??!)

# Stage 2   Skills training

# 2.1 Extending vocabulary

■ □ □ □ □ □ □

## Step 1  How do you feel about learning vocabulary?

1. Brigitte and Adel have different feelings about learning English vocabulary.

*I really like learning new words. I think it's so important if you want to express yourself well.*

Brigitte, Switzerland

*I don't think it's necessary to learn lots of new words. I can always get round it somehow if I don't know the exact word.*

Adel, Algeria

What are the positive and negative aspects of these two opinions about vocabulary learning?

2. How do *you* feel about learning English vocabulary?

3. Find out what other people in your group feel.

27

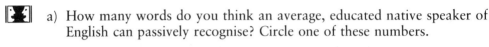

## Step 2 What do you know about English vocabulary?

### 1 Active and passive vocabulary

*I can understand English quite
well, but I can't say much.*

Sidsel, Norway

a) How many words do you think an average, educated native speaker of English can passively recognise? Circle one of these numbers.

2,000   5,000   10,000   20,000   50,000   200,000   500,000

b) How many words do you think an average educated native speaker of English can actively use? Circle one of these numbers.

2,000   5,000   10,000   20,000   50,000   200,000   500,000

Check your estimates for (a) and (b) with your teacher.

c) How many words do you think you know in your own language?

### 2 Knowing a word

a) What do you think 'knowing' a word means? Look at the following list:

i)     to understand it when it is written and/or spoken
ii)    to recall it when you need it
iii)   to use it with the correct meaning
iv)    to use it in a grammatically correct way
v)     to pronounce it correctly
vi)    to know which other words you can use with it
vii)   to spell it correctly
viii)  to use it in the right situation
ix)    to know if it has positive or negative associations

These points may not all be equally important to you for 'knowing' a particular word or phrase. Their importance may depend on whether you need to recognise a word passively or whether you want to use it actively.

b) Think of an English word or phrase you have met recently and decide which of points (i)–(ix) are important for you. Here are some examples:

*My word is 'propagation'. For me it is important to understand it when it is written – Point (i) – because my hobby is growing indoor plants and I have a book which gives me information on how to grow new plants from the ones I already have.*

Manjula, India (now living in Birmingham)

**SECRETS OF SUCCESS**

**Temperature:** Average warmth; not less than 45°F in winter.

**Light:** Not fussy; a well-lit spot away from direct sunlight is best.

**Water:** Water liberally from spring to autumn; sparingly in winter.

**Air Humidity:** Misting occasionally in summer is beneficial.

**Repotting:** Repot in spring if plant has started to lift out of the pot.

**Propagation:** Peg down plantlets in compost — cut stem when rooted. Alternatively divide plants at repotting time.

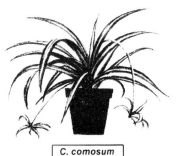

*C. comosum variegatum*

**Spider Plant (St. Bernard's Lily)**

From *The House Plant Expert* by Dr D. G. Hessayon

*My word is 'beetroot'. I'm allergic to it. If I eat it, I'm sick, so all of the points are important for me – except maybe Point (ix). I think 'beetroot' is not a word with positive or negative associations.*

Fumiko, Japan

c) Here is a list of words and phrases. Find out their meanings and then decide, for each one, which of points (i)–(ix) are important for you. (You may decide that you don't need or want to know some of this list at all.)

| | |
|---|---|
| widespread | Tradescantia |
| spokesperson | disgusting |
| What a pity! | to knit |
| bitch | screwdriver |

Compare your decisions with other class members.

d) What kinds of words do you think would be most useful for you to learn? Why?

■ ■ ■ ☐ ☐ ☐ ☐

# Step 3  How well are you doing?

### Introduction

Although you may think that it is your teacher's job to tell you how well you are doing, assessing yourself can be very useful because it can help you to rely on yourself in situations when your teacher is not with you. You can assess yourself in the following ways:

a) by asking yourself 'How well did I do?' in a specific practice activity or real-life situation, so you can identify your strong and weak points and plan your learning better;

b) by keeping records of work you have done so you can see the progress you are making.

The results of your self-assessment can then help you decide whether what you are doing is effective for you and identify what you need to work on next.

### 1  Points to assess

Before you can assess your vocabulary learning, you need to be clear about what aspects you want to assess. Look back at Step 2(2) 'Knowing a word', where you decided which points were important; you could base your assessment on some of these. You will find an example on page 32.

### 2  Test yourself in a practice activity

Read what Stig says about testing himself.

*I cover up the English in my vocabulary book, I look at the Swedish translation and try to write the English down again. Then I see how many I've got and give myself one mark for each correct word and half a mark if the spelling is wrong. If my score is low, I test myself again the next day after I've had time to look at the words again.*

Stig, Sweden

 Do you know of any good ways of testing yourself on vocabulary? For example:
– using two-sided cards
– making word networks (see Step 5)
– using word bags (see Step 5)

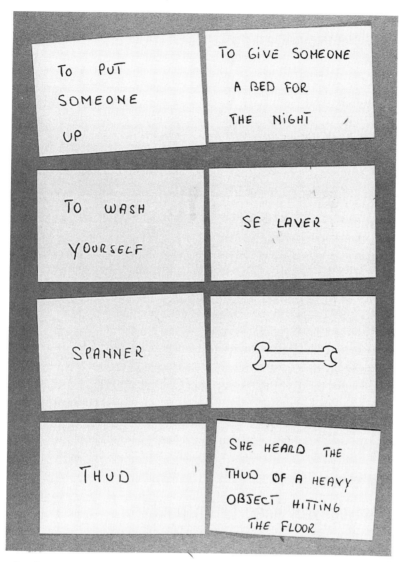

## 3   Assess your performance in a real-life situation

Read what Mimi says about assessing herself.

*Last week I was talking to a friend and the topic of accidents at nuclear power stations came up. I wanted to give my opinions but just didn't have the vocabulary to do this. I was frustrated and dissatisfied, so when I got home, I looked the words up in my dictionary and made a list of them.*

Mimi, Singapore

 Think of a real-life situation you have been in recently, where you needed to use English. Did you have any problems with vocabulary? What were they?

### 4 Examples

This is how Stig and Mimi assessed themselves.

Name: *Stig*

| Date | Activity/Situation | Points to assess | Assessment |
|------|--------------------|------------------|------------|
| *26.7.88* | *Testing vocabulary on washing machines for writing instructions* | *– spelling*<br>*– labelling parts of machine correctly* | *Poor!*<br>*Need more specific vocabulary.* |

Name: *Mimi*

| Date | Activity/Situation | Points to assess | Assessment |
|------|--------------------|------------------|------------|
| *26.7.88* | *Talking to Fred about nuclear accidents* | *Vocabulary* | *OK but:*<br>*– polite ways of interrupting*<br>*– special vocabulary for nuclear accidents* |

You will find a blank self-assessment chart on page 114 in the Appendix. You could use a copy of this to do your own self-assessment.

■ ■ ■ ■ □ □ □

## Step 4  What do you need to do next?

### Introduction

Language learning takes a lot of hard work and time. However, if you can set yourself realistic short-term aims, you will find it easier to manage your learning and see your progress. One way you could do this is to use a chart.

Name:

| What? | How? | When? | How long? | Done |
|-------|------|-------|-----------|------|
|       |      |       |           |      |

1. Look back at your self-assessment chart (Step 3).

2. Look at what you noted under *Assessment* and decide what points you need to work on next. Write these in the column marked *What?*. These are your short-term aims.

3. Decide how you can achieve each aim and describe this in the column marked *How?*.

4. Decide when you will do this and how much time you will spend on it and write these in the columns marked *When?* and *How long?*.

5. When you have achieved your aim, put a tick (✓) in the column marked *Done*.

You will find a blank chart for your own use on page 114 in the Appendix.

**Examples**

Here are examples of how Stig and Mimi set themselves short-term aims.

Name: *Stig*

| What? | How? | When? | How long? | Done |
|---|---|---|---|---|
| *Spelling* | *Copy – 10 times.* | *29.7.88* | *10 mins.* | ✓ |
| *More specific washing machine vocabulary* | *Read Manufacturer's Instructions in English and note down words.* | | *30 mins.* | ✓ |

Name: *Mimi*

| What? | How? | When? | How long? | Done |
|---|---|---|---|---|
| *Polite ways of interrupting* | *'Functions of English' Unit 5.* | *28.7.88* | *15 mins.* | ✓ |
| *Special vocabulary for nuclear accidents* | *Read newspaper articles about Chernobyl.* | | *1 hour* | ✓ |

■ ■ ■ ■ ■ □ □

## Step 5 How do you prefer to learn vocabulary?

### 1 Personal strategies

We interviewed some students to find out what strategies they use for learning new words.

*I have to see the word written down. If you just say it I can't remember it.*

Luis, Portugal

*I think I remember words best by listening and then repeating them aloud.*

Anne, Belgium

*I try to learn new words together with their translations.*

Leila, Tunisia

*I need to write the word several times before I remember it.*

Jia-Qi, China

*I think it's a good idea to learn vocabulary by topic, for example, types of furniture, parts of the car, because if I think back, some of them remind me of others.*

André, France

 How do *you* prefer to learn new words? Can you think of any other ways?

*Activity: Learning new words*

a) You have five minutes to learn some new words that your teacher will provide.
b) How many of the new words can you remember? Write them down.
c) How did you learn the words?

d) Who was the most successful learner in your group? How did he or she learn the words? Would this be a good strategy for you too?

## 2   Time to experiment – Grouping words

Research has shown that people often remember words in groups which have something in common. The way we group our words is always very personal.

*Activity: Common features*

a) Here are some words which have been sorted into groups. Can you see what each group has in common?

Group 1: shoe   shop   shout   shine   sheep
Group 2: greenhouse   breadboard   penknife
Group 3: biology   geology   psychology
Group 4: run   jump   hop   sprint   jog

b) Sort the following words into groups. When you have finished, find out if another learner can discover what your groups have in common.

walnut   melon   currant   tomato
blackberry   raspberry
chicken   banana
peach   gooseberry   chestnut   grapefruit
thyme
hazelnut   lemon   pear   turkey
strawberry   kitchen

How many different ways of grouping these words did your class use?

c) Can you think of any other ways of grouping the words in (b) that could help you to remember them? What are they?

35

*Activity: Word network*

Grouping words according to their *meanings* can be a useful way to remember them. Here is an example of one way of doing this.

a) Choose a topic, for example 'politics'. Write it in the middle of a blank sheet of paper.

b) What is the first word that comes into your mind which is connected in some way with it? (If the word is in your language, find out the English for it.) Write the English word anywhere you like on the paper and join it to the first word.

c) Continue in this way, adding new words as you think of them.

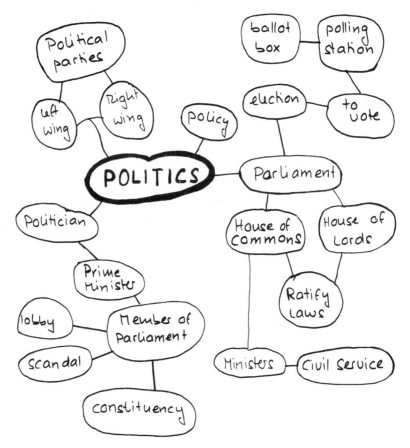

Each word network you create is unique because *you* have thought of the words, and made the connections. Your word network can be as large as you like.

If you decide to try this strategy, test yourself later on and you will probably be amazed at how many new words you can remember.

If you decide to use this strategy regularly, make sure you store your networks efficiently, for example, by topic. (See Step 7 for further details.)

### 3 Time to experiment – Making associations

*Activity: Word bag*

Research has also shown that people remember words by making associations in their minds.

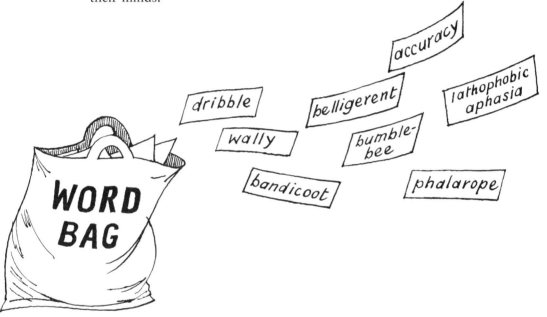

For this activity you will need a large plastic carrier bag and some small pieces of card.

a) When you meet a new word that you want to learn, write it, or cut it out and stick it, on to a piece of card.

b) Look at the word and try to recall the whole sentence and its meaning. Make up pictures/associations in your mind to help you remember it. Be imaginative!

c) Put the word in your word bag.

d) Later, take out a card. Look at the word on the card and try to recall its meaning. You will probably find that your picture/association will help you.

If you keep a separate record of each word in its original context, you can check you were right.

*Activity: Word tour*

a)  Think of a town or city you know well. Imagine that you are organising a sightseeing tour for tourists.

b)  Think of five places you would include on your tour and write down the order in which the tourists will visit them.

c)  Learn your tour off by heart so that you can picture it in your mind.

d)  Whenever you have five new English words to learn, imagine these words are the tourists on your tour and picture the words in the places on your tour, like this:

| *Tour:* Trafalgar Square | *Words to learn:* apron |
|---|---|
| Buckingham Palace | dustpan |
| Houses of Parliament | vacuum cleaner |
| Westminster Abbey | feather duster |
| Downing Street | broom |

–  Imagine Nelson (on his column in Trafalgar Square) wearing an apron.
–  Imagine the Queen brushing the floor in Buckingham Palace and using a dustpan.
–  Imagine a Member of Parliament vacuuming the corridors in the Houses of Parliament.
    Can you imagine pictures for the other words?

*Activity: Word clip*

For words that are difficult to picture in your mind, make up a story, like a video clip, in your mind. Imagine famous people acting in your video clip and doing or saying the words you want to remember.

## 4   Choose a new strategy

We suggest you experiment with new strategies for learning vocabulary in order to find the one(s) you prefer.

■ ■ ■ ■ ■ □

# Step 6 Do you need to build up your confidence?

**What can you do when you don't know a word?**

Listen to three people in a shop describing an object they want to buy but don't know the word for. Can you guess what the object is?

In a situation like this, there are several strategies you can use if you don't know the word. Can you think of any? Look at the chart below to see some examples.

- Listen again to the people on the cassette and tick (✓) the strategies you hear them using.
- Which strategy or combination of strategies do you think was the most effective and why?
- Can you think of any other strategies that may be effective? Add them to the list.

| *Strategies* | *Speaker 1* | *Speaker 2* | *Speaker 3* |
|---|---|---|---|
| i) using a foreign word | | | |
| ii) describing what it is for | | | |
| iii) describing what it looks like and what it is made of | | | |
| iv) using a word that is close in meaning | | | |
| v) inventing a new word or expression | | | |
| vi) using substitute words e.g. 'thingy' | | | |
| vii) other | | | |

*Activity: Shopping*

Try out some of the strategies from the chart.

a) Your teacher will give you and your partner some objects or pictures of objects that you need to buy. Do not show your objects to anyone else in the classroom.

b) You have five minutes to prepare your strategies for buying these objects (look back at page 39 for some ideas).

c) Give the objects back to your teacher.

d) Change partners. One of you is the shop assistant and the other the customer. The customer must try to buy his or her objects, using the strategies prepared in (b). The shop assistant must try to work out what the customer wants. Change roles. The first pair to finish their shopping are the winners.

e) How successful were your partner's strategies?

■ ■ ■ ■ ■ ■ ■

## Step 7   How do you organise your vocabulary learning?

Here are some suggestions from learners.

*I record new words in sentences on cassettes and listen to them regularly. I use different cassettes for different topics.*

Krystyna, Poland

*I am making a collage of advertisements, packet labels, etc. which have interesting or useful words on them. I stick them on the wall in my bedroom. Sometimes I use words from my collage to make word networks.*

Raya, India

*I have a three-step system. First I write new words down in a note book, then I transfer the words to a piece of paper and stick them on the wall in my office. If I don't know them after a week, I transfer them to new pieces of paper and stick them on my bedroom wall at home as well.*

Marie Ange, France

There are many different ways of collecting and organising vocabulary. How do you do this?

On pages 42 and 43 are some ways of organising vocabulary books. Which of these do you prefer and why?

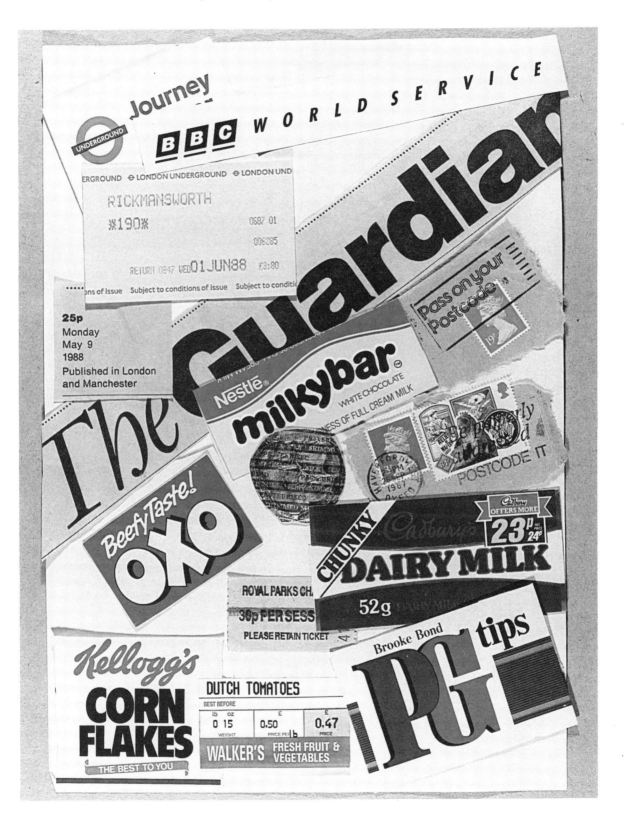

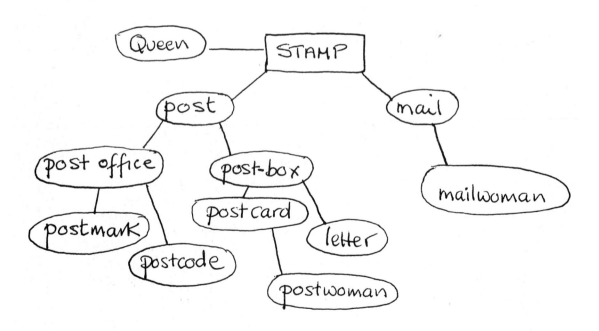

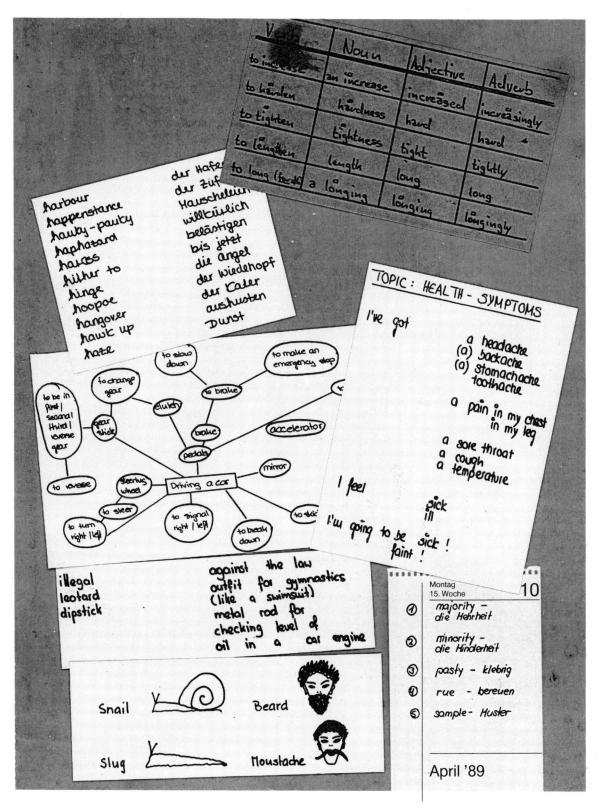

| Verb | Noun | Adjective | Adverb |
|---|---|---|---|
| to increase | an increase | increased | |
| to harden | hardness | increased | increasingly |
| to tighten | tightness | hard | hard |
| to lengthen | length | tight | tightly |
| to long (for) | a longing | long | long |
| | | longing | longingly |

harbour
happenstance
hanky-panky
haphazard
harass
hither to
hinge
hoopoe
hangover
hawk up
haze

der Hafe...
der Zuf...
Hauschelei...
willkürlich
belästigen
bis jetzt
die Angel
der Wiedehopf
der Kater
aushusten
Dunst

**TOPIC: HEALTH – SYMPTOMS**

I've got

- (a) headache
- (a) backache
- (a) stomachache
- toothache

a pain in my chest
in my leg

a sore throat
a cough
a temperature

I feel

sick
ill

I'm going to be sick!
faint!

Driving a car mind-map: to slow down, to make an emergency stop, to change gear, to brake, clutch, brake, accelerator, to be in first / second / third / reverse gear, gear stick, pedals, mirror, steering wheel, to reverse, to steer, to turn right / left, to signal right / left, to break down, Driving a car

illegal
leotard
dipstick

against the law
outfit for gymnastics
(like a swimsuit)
metal rod for
checking level of
oil in a car engine

Snail

Slug

Beard

Moustache

Montag
15. Woche                    **10**

① majority –
   die Mehrheit
② minority –
   die Minderheit
③ pasty – klebrig
④ rue – bereuen
⑤ sample – Muster

April '89

# 2.2 Dealing with grammar

■ □ □ □ □ □ □

## Step 1  How do you feel about learning grammar?

1. Look at what these learners say about English grammar.

*I think English is difficult. It's illogical. There are too many exceptions.*

Marjeta, Yugoslavia

*I don't think grammar's the most important thing. There are other things, like vocabulary, body language, culture and so on which are just as important to know about.*

Wolfgang, Austria

*I don't think you can learn to speak a language without learning the grammar first.*

Boniface, Martinique

*I hate it. I think it's boring but I suppose it's necessary.*

Filippo, Italy

   2. How do *you* feel about learning English grammar?

   3. Find out what other people in your group feel.

■ ■ ☐ ☐ ☐ ☐

# Step 2  What do you know about English grammar?

 **1  Languages are different**

a) The grammar systems of languages can vary from being quite similar to each other to being very different from each other. How similar or different is the grammar of your language compared with the grammar of English? Can you give some examples like these?

*In my language (Russian), we have no verb 'to be' in the present tense. We say 'I Russian' ( я русская ).*

Natasha, Soviet Union

*In French we often put adjectives after the noun, like this: 'A woman very rich'* (une femme très riche).

Jacques, Québec

*In Vietnamese we don't have present, future or past forms of verbs at all. Sometimes we just put a little word in front of a verb to show if it is present, future or past, like this: sẽ before a verb means future.*

Vinh, Vietnam

*German nouns can be masculine* (Der Mann), *feminine* (Die Frau) *or neuter* (Das Haus).

Ursula, GDR

Listen to the cassette for some more examples.

b) Dutch, for example, is relatively similar to English, but Japanese is very different. What is your feeling about your own language? Where would you place it on this line? Why?

very similar – – – – – – – – – – – – – – – – – – – – – – – very different

English    Dutch                                            Japanese

*Very similar:* Lucky you! You probably will not find English grammar too difficult to learn.
*Very different:* Be prepared to spend more time and effort learning English grammar and to meet some new ways of expressing ideas that may seem strange to you.

46

## 2  What is grammar?

The following diagram shows how the grammar of English can be divided into three main areas.

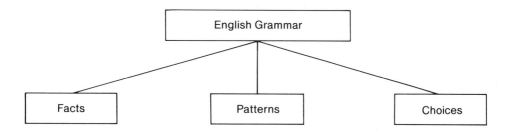

**Facts**: this part of grammar is simply fact, for example:

**plurals: woman/women; wife/wives**
**verb forms: I write / I wrote / I have written**

The only thing you can do with facts is learn them.

**Patterns**: this part of grammar shows how some language falls into certain patterns, for example:

| What | do<br>does<br>do | you<br>he<br>you | do?<br>think?<br>want? |
|------|------|------|------|

We can use this pattern to make new questions beginning with 'what', for example:

| What | do<br>did<br>do | you<br>you<br>they | like?<br>prefer?<br>prefer? |
|------|------|------|------|

Patterns need to be learnt. Learning patterns can save you time and effort because from one pattern you can generate new language.

**Choices**: In any situation you may have a choice of language forms, both or all of which are grammatically correct. This choice may be completely free, for example:

'I've played tennis since I was a child.'
'I've been playing tennis since I was a child.'

Or it may depend on what you really mean or how you feel at the time, for example:

'She always loses her keys.'
'She's always losing her keys.'

You are likely to sound more irritated if you choose the second sentence from the pair on page 47, although this could depend on other factors such as intonation. The differences in meaning can be very small and you need to develop a deeper understanding of how meaning and grammar are related. This can take time, but the more you read and listen to English, the easier it will become. It can be very interesting and useful to discuss the problems of choice with others.

### Activity: Using a pattern

 How many sentences can you generate from this pattern? You have three minutes.

*I love jogging in the evening.*
*I love swimming in the morning.*

 Now compare your lists around the class.
     You could build up a Pattern Bank so that you can generate new language (see Step 5).

■ ■ ■ ☐ ☐ ☐ ☐

## Step 3   How well are you doing?

If you are doing a Step 3 for the first time, read the Introduction on page 30 in *2.1 Extending vocabulary*.

### 1   Points to assess

Before you can assess your use of grammar, you need to be clear about what exactly you want to assess.

 a) First of all you need to consider what kinds of grammatical mistakes you think are serious. Some are more serious than others because they make the meaning unclear and can cause confusion. Look at the examples of spoken English below. In each one there is a sentence (marked*) with a mistake. Decide how serious you think each mistake is and why. Discuss.

   i)   A: What does your brother do?

        B: *He work in a factory.

   ii)  *Where you go for your holiday?

   iii) A: What's the matter?

        B: *I've been cutting my finger.

   iv)  A: Are you going swimming?

        B: *It depends from the weather.

   v)   *What means 'flabbergasted'?

b) Do you think it is more important to be correct when writing or when speaking? Why?

c) When you have thought about which mistakes are serious and whether you are going to assess your speaking or writing, you can choose particular points to assess. Here are some suggestions:
– tenses e.g. past tenses, present tenses
– prepositions e.g. of direction, of location
– question tags e.g. It's a nice day, *isn't it?*
– word order
– comparatives e.g. She's *taller* than Fred.
– superlatives e.g. She's *the tallest* in the class.
etc.
Select only two or three of these at a time.

## 2 Test yourself in a practice activity

Read about how Delia tests herself on grammar.

*I've got a book of grammar
exercises with answers at the
back, so I can easily give myself
tests on the things I find tricky,
like the conditionals in English.*

Delia, Ecuador

 Do you know of any good materials for testing yourself in this way?

## 3 Assess your performance in a real-life situation

Read about how Khaled assesses his performance.

*English is very important for my
work at the airport. It is very
important to get tenses right. I
record conversations in my office
with English-speaking colleagues
and listen to find out how well I
did afterwards.*

Khaled, Kuwait

 Think of a real-life situation you have been in recently, where you needed to use English. Did you have any problems with your grammar? What were they?

49

**4 Examples**

This is how Delia and Khaled assessed themselves.

Name: *Delia*

| Date | Activity/Situation | Points to assess | Assessment |
|------|-------------------|------------------|------------|
| *1.8.88* | *Testing myself Unit 37 'English Grammar in Use'* | *Correctness in 'if' and 'wish' sentences* | *50% 'wish' sentences – especially 'I wish I weren't so stupid.'* |

Name: *Khaled*

| Date | Activity/Situation | Points to assess | Assessment |
|------|-------------------|------------------|------------|
| *2.8.88* | *Conversation with Norman about last week's work schedule* | *Correct use of past tenses* | *Getting better, but not good enough. Past Perfect – 'I had told him not to do it, but he did it again'.* |

You will find a blank self-assessment chart on page 114 in the Appendix. You could use a copy of this to do your own self-assessment.

■ ■ ■ ■ □ □ □

# Step 4 What do you need to do next?

If you are doing a Step 4 for the first time, read the Introduction on page 32 of *2.1 Extending vocabulary*.

**Examples**

Here are examples of how Delia and Khaled set themselves short-term aims:

Name: *Delia*

| What? | How? | When? | How long? | Done |
|-------|------|-------|-----------|------|
| *'wish' sentences* | *Revise Unit 37 'English Grammar in Use'. Read other grammar books.* | *3.8.88* | *30 mins.* | ✓ |

Name: *Khaled*

| What? | How? | When? | How long? | Done |
|---|---|---|---|---|
| *Past perfect* | *Read newspaper articles and notice how Past Perfect is used.* | *3.8.88* | *45 mins.* | ✓ |

You will find a blank chart which you can copy for your own use on page 115 in the Appendix.

■ ■ ■ ■ ■ ☐ ☐

## Step 5   How do you prefer to learn grammar?

### 1   Personal strategies

We asked some students what strategies they use for dealing with grammar.

*I ask my American boyfriend to tell me every time I make a particular grammar mistake – like when I get questions wrong.*

Leah, Philippines

*I choose a grammar point of the week, like 'passives' or 'second conditionals' and then I look in newspapers or magazines for examples. I cut the paragraphs out and keep them in a scrapbook. I see if my examples fit the notes in my grammar books.*

Pedro, Costa Rica

*To help myself learn new rules, I use a grammar book with exercises. I don't read the explanations because I don't understand them. Instead I try a question in an exercise and then look up the answer immediately. This helps me do the next question. I check the answer after each question. I learn as I go.*

Yasmeen, Pakistan

How do *you* prefer to learn grammar? Can you think of any other ways?

**2   Suggestions**

a) Build up a *Pattern Bank* so you can collect examples and generate new ones. Try out new examples on a native speaker from time to time. Read and listen to English as much as possible for examples of how grammar is used.

PASSIVES

The seized guns were handed over by the Customs men to the police.

Daily Mail  28.8.86

The registered letter was delivered by the messenger to the boss.

The sick parrot was taken by Mr. Brown to the vet's.

"I was followed by 2 man" (quote from TV programme)

He was chased by a dog

b) Discuss grammar:
   – in class
   – with other learners
   – with native speakers

Listen to Chen and Kasuko discussing the following sentences:

'I lived in London for ten years.'
'I have lived in London for ten years.'

**3   Choose a new strategy**

We suggest you experiment with new strategies for dealing with grammar in order to find the one(s) you prefer.

# Step 6  Do you need to build up your confidence?

**Discovering the pattern or rule**

The explanations in some grammar books can be confusing and difficult to understand. There are other ways of learning to understand grammar, but you need to be prepared to experiment. Try to discover grammar 'rules' by yourself or together with other learners, like this:

– Look at two or three examples of language illustrating the same grammar point. (You can find examples in grammar books or get them from your teacher.)

– Try to work out the rule.
– When you are satisfied with your rule, look at some more examples to see if
  they fit it.
– If they don't, try to adapt your rule.
– Continue to collect examples from time to time and check that they fit your
  rule. You may need to adapt your rule again.
  By discussing the problem and trying to work it out for yourself, you are
  helping yourself to get a better understanding of the grammar. What is more,
  the rule will probably become easier to remember.

### Activity: Some and any

 a) Look at these examples of the use of *some* and *any*.

> Have you got any money?
> I haven't got any money.
> I've got some money.

What do you think the rule is? Write it down.

 b) Now ask your teacher for some more examples with *some* and *any*. Check
   your rule and adapt it if necessary.

 ### Activity: The human computer

 In this game you can build up your confidence in using a new grammar pattern
or rule. You can take a chance and try to test the human computer.
   Your teacher will become the human computer, which is programmed to give
only *correct* examples of a grammar point, for example, the passive in the
simple past: 'She *was awarded* a prize.'

53

When the 'computer' is ready you can test it by giving sentences which are either right or wrong. In the following examples, wrong sentences are marked*. The 'computer' should always give the correct version, like this:

Learner 1:          *She is awarded a prize.
Human computer:   She was awarded a prize.

Learner 2:          The flowers were picked.
Human computer:   The flowers were picked.

Learner 3:          *The telephone was rung.
Human computer:   She was telephoned.

Listen to the cassette for an example of how to play this game. Always listen carefully to the answers given by the 'computer', to check if your sentence was correct or not. After you have had some practice, one of you could become the human computer.

■ ■ ■ ■ ■ ■

## Step 7  How do you organise your grammar learning?

Here are some ways of organising your grammar learning.

1. Organise a regular time for practising grammar.

2. Get a grammar book you find easy to use (see 1.4(2) page 13).

3. Regularly review the grammar covered in your class or course book.

4. Listen to and read English as much as possible.

5. Keep a Pattern Bank (see Step 5).

6. Form a 'Grammar Club' to discuss grammatical problems.

# 2.3 Listening

■ ☐ ☐ ☐ ☐ ☐

## Step 1   How do you feel about listening to English?

1. These learners told us what they think about listening to English.

*I get irritated because I can't always understand everything.*

Somsamai, Thailand

*I love listening to the sound of English – I think it's a beautiful language.*

Soraya, Ivory Coast

*I don't mind if I don't understand everything, the main ideas are enough and the way people look and move helps me to understand too.*

Paul, Netherlands

 2. How do *you* feel about listening to English?

 3. Find out what other people in your group feel.

■ ■ □ □ □ □ □

## Step 2 What do you know about listening to English?

**1 Listening to native speakers of English**

Listen to Marie-Claude asking for directions in London. What problems is she having?

Do you ever have any problems like Marie-Claude? If so, this is probably because English is a stress-timed language. This means that spoken English has a regular beat which affects the way some words are pronounced.

– Listen to the four sentences on the cassette.

| 1 | 2 | 3 | 4 |
|---|---|---|---|
| 1 and | 2 and | 3 and | 4 |
| 1 and a | 2 and a | 3 and a | 4 |
| 1 and then a | 2 and then a | 3 and then a | 4 |

– Can you hear the beats? Where are they? These are the stressed words.
– Listen again. What happens to the pronounciation of the words between the stressed words? Is your language like this?

– Listen to Marie-Claude again. What are the first directions she gets, starting from 'Well look,' to '. . . OK'? Which words are stressed? What kinds of words are usually stressed in spoken English?
– How can this information about stress help you when you are listening to spoken English?

*Activity: Guessing what a conversation is about*

Even if you can't hear or understand *all* the words when you are listening to English, you can usually understand the general meaning of a conversation if you listen for the stressed words.

a) Look at the pictures on page 57. You will hear three short conversations. As you listen, match each conversation with one of the pictures by putting a number in the box. For example, you should write 1 on the picture that you think matches the first conversation that you hear. (Three pictures will not have numbers.)

b) Compare answers.

c) Listen again and make a note of the words in each conversation that helped you to guess what it was about.

d) Which conversation did you find the easiest to understand? Why?

e) Which conversation did you find the most difficult to understand? Why?

57

## 2  Listening strategies

A good listener varies his or her listening strategy according to *why*  he or she is listening. Having a reason for listening helps you to focus on what you need or want to listen for.

When might you use the following strategies?

*Listening for gist:* to find out the general ideas.

*Selecting and rejecting:* having a specific point in mind and just listening for that.

 Can you think of a situation where you really need to understand every word of what you are listening to? Give an example if you can.

 *Activity: Reasons for listening*

For each of the following situations, listen to the cassette and then discuss which listening strategies you used and why.

a) You are inviting some friends for a meal tonight, but you don't know what to cook. You think you might try the radio recipe. You tune in and listen ...

b) You want to go and see *A Handful of Dust* at your local cinema. Decide when you can go and listen to the recorded message to find out what time it's on.

**Haymarket, Chelsea, Oxford Street, Screen on Baker Street, Acton Screen.**
**A HANDFUL OF DUST (PG)** Brilliant adaptation of Evelyn Waugh's semi- autiobiographical satire of the social and selfish in the 1930s, impeccably played by Kristin Scott Thomas, Rupert Graves, James Wilby, Anjelica Huston, Judi Dench, Alec Guinness. Dir Charles Sturridge GB 1988. 105 minutes. **Cannons Shaftesbury Avenue and Fulham Road, Screen on the Hill,** till Aug 11.

**HAWKS (15).** Grotesque, would-be comedy of two terminal patients absconding

min
**THI**
con
insp
the
Ra
Ca
Kei
**THE**
Brilli
cult
Russia

■ ■ ■ ☐ ☐ ☐ ☐

# Step 3  How well are you doing?

If you are doing a Step 3 for the first time, read the Introduction on page 30 in *2.1 Extending vocabulary.*

### 1  Points to assess

Before you try to assess your listening comprehension, it is helpful to think about some of the factors that help you to understand or prevent you from understanding what is being said. For example:

a) *who you were listening to* – Was the person speaking too fast for me?
   – Was the accent a familiar one?

b) *the topic* – Did I know much about the topic?
   – Was I interested in the topic?
   – Did I know most of the words?

c) *the situation* – Could I see the speaker?
   – Could I talk to the speaker?
   – Were there several people speaking at the same time?
   – Were there several speakers with similar voices?
   – Was there any background noise or interference?

d) *you* – Was I clear about my reason for listening?
   – Did I use the best listening strategy?
   – Did I feel tired/impatient, etc?

When you assess your listening comprehension you are really assessing how you cope with these factors. Remember that it is a good idea to concentrate on only one or two of them at a time.

### 2  Test yourself in a practice activity

Read what Micheline says. What does she do to test herself?

*I've found the best way for me to test my listening is to buy one of those cassettes especially for practising your listening, and the book that goes with it. I like the activities where you have to do something while you're listening, for example, match a description to a picture or follow directions on a map or something like that. Then I can check in the answers to see if I'm right. Sometimes I look at the tapescripts when I'm really stuck and this helps me see where I had problems.*

Micheline, France

 Do you know of any other good ways of testing yourself?

59

### 3  Assess your performance in a real-life situation

Read what Santiago says. How does he assess how well he understood?

*I sometimes record parts of my
conversations with my English
friend and then I take the
recording home and listen for the
times when I didn't understand
and I try to analyse why.*

Santiago, Mexico

Think of a real-life situation you have been in recently where you needed to understand spoken English. How well did you do?

### 4  Examples

This is how Micheline and Santiago assessed themselves.

Name: *Micheline*

| Date | Activity/Situation | Points to assess | Assessment |
|------|-------------------|------------------|------------|
| *31.7.88* | *'Task Listening' Unit 23 'Following instructions'* | *Listening for the main idea (gist)* | *Not satisfied. Recognising important words (stressed words).* |

Name: *Santiago*

| Date | Activity/Situation | Points to assess | Assessment |
|------|-------------------|------------------|------------|
| *3.8.88* | *Talking to Carrie about feminism* | *Listening for details* | *Not satisfied. Understanding fast speech!* |

You will find a blank self-assessment chart on page 114 in the Appendix. You could use a copy of this to do your own self-assessment.

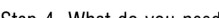

# Step 4  What do you need to do next?

If you are doing a Step 4 for the first time, read the Introduction on page 32 of *2.1 Extending vocabulary.*

**Examples**

Here are examples of how Micheline and Santiago set themselves short-term aims.

Name: *Micheline*

| What? | How? | When? | How long? | Done |
|-------|------|-------|-----------|------|
| *Recognising important words (stressed words)* | *Listen to some recordings from 'What a Story' then write a short summary.* | *5.8.88* | *1 hour* | ✓ |

Name: *Santiago*

| What? | How? | When? | How long? | Done |
|-------|------|-------|-----------|------|
| *Understanding fast speech* | *Listen to Capital Radio phone-in.* | *9 a.m. 5.8.88* | *1 hour* | ✓ |

You will find a blank chart which you can copy for your own use on page 115 in the Appendix.

■ ■ ■ ■ □ □

# Step 5   How do you prefer to practise your listening?

### 1   Personal strategies

We interviewed some students to find out what strategies they use for practising their listening. This is what they said.

*I record* Follow Me *from the TV on my video recorder. Then I watch it several times. When I'm familiar with it, I record the sound track on to a cassette and then listen to this while I'm jogging. I can see the pictures in my mind.*

Günter, W. Germany

*When I visit England I like to travel on buses and try to listen to people's conversations. Sometimes it's really funny and I hear a lot of slang.*

Mimma, Finland

*I really love pop music and try to listen to songs in English again and again until I understand as much as possible.*

Marisol, Spain

*Sometimes we get English language films on TV in Austria with German subtitles. After watching the film for a little while to find out the story, I cover up the subtitles with a piece of paper for a few minutes at a time and try to follow the film.*

Franz, Austria

   How do *you* prefer to practise your listening? Can you think of any other ways?

### 2 Time to experiment

 *Activity: How to take control*

 a) Listen to Jane explaining to her friend how to get to her house. What strategies does he use to take control of the situation and make sure he understands? Can you think of any others?

b) Your teacher will dictate a message to you. Practise the strategies you have just heard to make sure you write the message down correctly.

### 3 Choose a new strategy

We suggest you experiment with new strategies for practising your listening in order to find the one(s) you prefer.

---

■ ■ ■ ■ ■ □

# Step 6 Do you need to build up your confidence?

### 1 Preparing and predicting

Preparing yourself before listening and training yourself to predict can build up your confidence and help you to understand more. This is what one learner told us.

*Before I listen to the news in*
*English, I try to read the*
*headlines in the newspaper first.*

Jordi, Spain

*Activity: Listening to the news*

If you have the opportunity to listen to the news in English, this activity will give you practice in preparing yourself for listening and in the strategy of selecting and rejecting (see page 58).

a) *Before listening:* prepare yourself by doing one of the following:
   – listen to the news in your own language
   – look at a newspaper in your own language
   – look at a newspaper in English
   Make a list of the topics you think will probably be presented on the news programme.
   Choose the two topics that you are most interested in and make brief notes about what you think will be said about them.

b) *While listening:* listen for the two news items you selected to check your predictions.

## 2 How we predict

When you listen to a person speaking your own language, in many situations you can be one step ahead of the speaker. You can very often predict what that person is going to say next – perhaps not always the exact words, but at least the main ideas. Have you ever found yourself finishing other people's sentences for them? This is often something we do without even thinking about it.

The more you can predict, the easier it becomes to understand – in a foreign language too. In fact, you will probably be surprised at how much you can predict in English. Train yourself to predict as much as possible. Do this consciously.

There are many things which can help you to predict while you are listening, for example:

*how much you know about:* the topic
the situation
the country in which the language is spoken

*signals* such as: 'I'm afraid that . . .' (signals something negative will follow)
'There's one point I'd like to make . . .' (signals an opinion will follow)

*connectors* such as: 'Although . . .'
'On the one hand . . . on the other hand . . .'
(signal the presentation of two contrasting ideas)

*sequencers* such as: 'Firstly . . .'
'Secondly . . .'
'Next . . .'
'Lastly . . .'

*intonation*, for example: when presenting a list, rising intonation signals that more items will follow and a falling intonation signals the end of the list:

'I'd like to buy some eggs, cheese, tomatoes and a cake.'

### Activity: Can you predict in English?

a) Listen to two unfinished sentences on the cassette. What do you think comes next? Listen to the complete sentences to check your guesses.

b) Now listen to the other speakers on the cassette and predict what they are going to say next. Note down your ideas and then compare them around the class.

c) Listen to the complete versions on the cassette to check your predictions. What things helped you to predict?

64

■■■■■■

## Step 7 How do you organise your listening practice?

Here are some ways of organising your listening practice.

1. Organise a regular time for listening practice.

2. To support your listening library (see page 15), collect articles from magazines and newspapers on the same or similar topics.

3. Read reviews of films, TV programmes, etc. either in English or in your own language, before listening or watching.

4. Keep programme guides and reviews for radio/TV programmes.

5. Get a cassette 'pen-friend'.*

6. Form a listening club so you can exchange cassettes and other listening materials with friends.

*A friend you will correspond with by cassette instead of by letter.

---

*Warning!*

There is almost certainly a *Copyright* law where you live.
Find out whether it is *legal* for you to make
recordings of broadcasts or published materials.

---

## 2.4 Speaking

■ □ □ □ □ □

### Step 1 How do you feel about speaking English?

1. These learners told us how they feel about speaking English.

*I want my English to be perfect
and I always try very hard to be
correct when I speak English. I
hate making mistakes and I want
to be corrected when I do.*

Herbert, W. Germany

*I'm sure I make a lot of mistakes
when I speak – but I no care –
the people they understand me –
mostly.*

Purificacion, Spain

*I think my accent in English is
terrible, but my teacher says it's
OK. I don't know why he says
this – I think if you try to learn
English, you should try to sound
like an English person.*

Vladimir, Yugoslavia

*I feel strange when I speak
English – like a different person.
I feel like I'm acting. I even think
my voice changes.*

Maria Elena, Colombia

*I think British English is the
best – I only want to learn
that.*

Valérie, French Guiana

2. How do *you* feel about speaking English?

3. Find out what other people in your group feel.

■ ■ □ □ □ □ □

# Step 2  What do you know about speaking English?

Countries in which English is the mother tongue

Countries in which English has official or semi-official
status as a language of national affairs

## 2.4 Speaking

### 1 English as a world language

a) Do you know how many people in the world speak English
   i)  as their first language?
   ii) as a second language?

b) Do you know in which countries English is used as an official language?

c) In each English-speaking country there are usually many different accents and dialects. However, there is usually a standard pronunciation which is understood wherever you go in that country. Listen to some examples of speakers from different English-speaking countries. Can you identify the accents? Number the accents in the order in which you hear them.

| | | | |
|---|---|---|---|
| 'Irish' English | ☐ | Australian English | ☐ |
| Indian English | ☐ | Nigerian English | ☐ |
| 'English' English | ☐ | US English | ☐ |

What differences did you hear between the accents?

d) There are many varieties of English in the world. The variety you choose to speak will depend on some or all of the following:
   – where you live
   – who you will be speaking English to
   – your personal interest in the country and its culture

*I work for an export company in Tokyo and we have much business with America, so I learn American English.*

Keiko, Japan

What kind of English do you want to speak and why?

### 2 Pronunciation

People from different non-English speaking countries have different pronunciation problems when speaking English.

For example, Spanish speakers may find it difficult to make a difference between /v/ and /b/ in English because in Spanish the letters *v* and *b* are pronounced in almost the same way. In some parts of southern China people often pronounce the English letter *r* as *l* because the sound /r/ does not exist in their language. They use the nearest sound to it from their language.

Make a list of some of the pronunciation problems typical of speakers of your language when speaking English and exchange information with the rest of the class.

**3 Stress**

*Syllables*

English words with two or more syllables usually have a stress on one of these syllables. Listen to the examples:

probably    doctor    chocolate

a) Listen to the following words on the cassette and mark the stressed syllables.

banana          photographer

area            advertisement

photograph

b) Now listen again to these words. Notice the pronunciation of the *unstressed* syllables.

c) Listen and repeat. Notice how important it is to get your stress right. Try putting the stress in a different place: a native speaker of English might not be able to understand the word.

When you are learning new words to use when speaking, make sure you know where the stress is and how to pronounce the word. You can get help from:

— a native speaker
— your teacher
— your dictionary

*Words in sentences*

By stressing different words in a sentence you can change its focus. Listen to the examples on the cassette.

I saw *John* yesterday (not Fred)
I saw John *yesterday* (not today)

 In the following example sentence, by stressing a different word you can answer different questions. Learner A asks the questions and learner B answers with the example sentence, stressing the appropriate word. Then change so that B asks the questions.

| *Questions:* | *Example sentence:* |
|---|---|
| i)  Who gave Jackie the bicycle? | David gave Jackie the bicycle. |
| ii)  How did Jackie get the bicycle? | |
| iii)  Who did David give the bicycle to? | |
| iv)  Which present did David give Jackie? | |

Now listen to the cassette to check if your stress was correct.

## 4   Intonation

Intonation is the way your voice rises or falls when you speak English. It can indicate:
– what the speaker means
– how the speaker feels
Listen to the example:

A: Jean, can you bring me the newspaper please?
B: Sorry?
(Jean means 'I didn't hear you, could you say that again please?')

 Now listen to these three short conversations. For each one, decide what the second speaker means, or how the second speaker feels.

i)   A: Ow! My foot!
     B: Oh, sorry!
ii)  A: Let's go to the cinema.
     B: Oh all right!
iii) A: Let's go to the cinema.
     B: Oh all right.

When you are learning to say phrases or sentences in English, try to copy the intonation.

## 5   Features of spoken English

a) What are some of the main differences between written and spoken English? Study this example. Tracey is inviting a friend to a party.
   i) Look at the written invitation.
   ii) Listen to the cassette.

What differences did you notice? Add them to these lists.

| Written | Spoken |
|---|---|
| formal abbreviations | informal repetition |

b) Both written and spoken English can vary in style from formal to informal. The level of formality depends, for example, on:

   i)   *who* you are communicating with and what your relationship with that person is e.g. your boss, your teacher, a close friend, a relative, a stranger

   ii)  *the situation* e.g. in a restaurant, at a formal business meeting, at home

   iii) *the topic* e.g. football, politics, a bank loan

   iv)  *your reason for speaking* e.g. to complain, to give advice, to invite, to disagree, to request

   v)   *your mood* e.g. happy, relaxed, anxious, irritated, very angry

   These factors influence the language, that is the vocabulary and structures that a native speaker chooses.

c) Listen to the conversations on the cassette and answer the questions in the chart.

|  | Conversation 1 | Conversation 2 | Conversation 3 |
|---|---|---|---|
| What is the relationship between the speakers? |  |  |  |
| Where are they? |  |  |  |
| What is the topic? |  |  |  |
| What are their reasons for speaking? |  |  |  |
| How do they feel? |  |  |  |

d) How many different ways can you ask somebody to be quiet? Make a list, starting with the most formal and finishing with the most informal. Then compare your ideas.

■ ■ ■ ☐ ☐ ☐ ☐

# Step 3  How well are you doing?

If you are doing a Step 3 for the first time, read the Introduction on page 30 in *2.1 Extending vocabulary.*

## 1  Points to assess

Before you can assess your speaking, you must be clear about what aspect(s) you want to assess. Firstly, are you going to focus on your accuracy or your fluency or both? Your choice of points to assess will probably also depend on:
– your strong and weak points in speaking
– your personal level of satisfaction with the way you speak
– your long-term aims e.g. to pass an oral examination, to give speeches at conferences, to visit your cousin in Dallas.

*Focus on accuracy*

This can be broken down into very specific points, from which you can select what you want to focus on. Here are some suggestions:

a) *Vocabulary,* for example:
correctness: Did I use the right words?
range: Did I use only a limited range of words?

b) *Grammar,* for example:
tenses: Did I use the right tense?
prepositions: Did I use the right prepositions?
question tags: Did I use the right question tags?

c) *Style:* Was I formal/informal enough? etc.

d) *Pronunciation of sounds:* Did I have a problem with a particular sound? e.g. /θ/ as in'think', /ɪ/ as in 'sit', or /ə/ as in 'doctor'.

e) *Stress:* Did I stress syllables/words correctly?

f) *Intonation:* How did I sound?
– polite?
– friendly?
– aggressive?
etc.

*Focus on fluency*

In this case, you are not concerned with assessing the correctness of specific points, but with the general effect of your spoken English.
Here are some suggestions:

a) *Meaning:* Was my meaning clear?

b) *Spontaneity:* Did I hesitate too much?
Was my speech slow and laboured?

*Activity: Describing a photograph*

Try this activity to help you assess spoken English.

  a) You will hear two different learners (A and B) talking about the photograph below. Work in pairs or groups. Before listening, choose one point to assess from the lists on page 72.

b) Listen to learner A. How well did she do?

 c) Discuss your opinion with the rest of the class.

d) Do the same for learner B.

*Activity: Recording yourself*

This activity will give you practice in assessing your spoken English, using points you have selected from the lists on page 72.

 a) Work in pairs. Your teacher will give each of you a picture or photograph to talk about. Take it in turns to record yourselves. (If you are working alone, imagine you are talking to another person.)

b) Listen to your recording. How well did you do?

c) Discuss your assessment with other learners who have listened to your recording.

## 2   Test yourself in a practice activity

Read Jürgen's suggestion for testing himself.

*I'm working on my pronunciation and stress at the moment – I record myself in simple imaginary role plays, for example in a shop. Then I listen and note my difficulties. I can usually find helpful pronunciation exercises in* Ship or Sheep, *and for stress my teacher recommended* Elements of Pronunciation.

Jürgen, W. Germany

Do you know of any other good ways of testing yourself?

## 3   Assess your performance in a real-life situation

Read what Santiago says about assessing himself.

*I record conversations with my English friends and then take them home so that I can listen to myself. At the moment, I'm trying to improve my fluency. Last week I hesitated too much, I said 'er' and 'um' too much and sometimes there was a long silence. So, I've been recording myself playing* Just a Minute *on my own.* (See Step 6.)

Santiago, Mexico

Think of a real-life situation you have been in recently where you needed to speak English. Did you have any problems? What were they?

## 4   Examples

This is how Jürgen and Santiago assessed themselves.

Name: *Jürgen*

| Date | Activity/Situation | Points to assess | Assessment |
|---|---|---|---|
| *22.3.88* | *Role playing – buying groceries* | *Pronunciation* | *Not satisfied! Couldn't say 'juice' or 'other'.* |

Name: *Santiago*

| Date | Activity/Situation | Points to assess | Assessment |
|------|--------------------|------------------|------------|
| *3.3.88* | *Talking to Carrie about feminism* | *Fluency* | *Not good. Being spontaneous, not hesitating so much.* |

You will find a blank self-assessment chart on page 114 in the Appendix. You could use a copy of this to do your own self-assessment.

■ ■ ■ ■ □ □ □

## Step 4   What do you need to do next?

If you are doing a Step 4 for the first time, read the Introduction on page 32 of *2.1 Extending vocabulary.*

### Examples

Here are examples of how Jürgen and Santiago set themselves short-term aims.

Name: *Jürgen*

| What? | How? | When? | How long? | Done |
|-------|------|-------|-----------|------|
| *Practise sounds: 'juice' 'other'* | *'Ship or Sheep' Units 35 & 42: listen and repeat.* | *23.3.88* | *10 mins.* | ✓ |

Name: *Santiago*

| What? | How? | When? | How long? | Done |
|-------|------|-------|-----------|------|
| *Practising being spontaneous* | *Record myself playing 'Just a Minute' and listen.* | *5.8.88* | *15 mins.* | ✓ |

You will find a blank chart which you can copy for your own use on page 115 in the Appendix.

■ ■ ■ ■ □ □

# Step 5  How do you prefer to practise your speaking?

### 1  Personal strategies

We interviewed some students to find out what strategies they use for practising their speaking. Here is what they said.

*I record myself reading aloud for pronunciation practice.*

Gizella, Hungary

*I've started an English language club and once a month we meet and talk English together.*

Gaby, Mexico

*I pretend I have an English friend with me and have imaginary conversations with her.*

Alphonsine, Congo

*I record my letter on cassette now for my pen-friend in Scotland.*

Carmen, Brazil

How do *you* prefer to practise your speaking? Can you think of any other ways?

### 2 Time to experiment

*Activity: Problem solving*

Think about the kinds of problems you might have when speaking a foreign language on the telephone. Can you think of any strategies you could use to improve your telephone techniques?

a) Gail often needs to make or answer telephone calls in French. You will hear her talking about her 'telephone strategy'. Here are some words she uses. Can you guess what her strategy is to improve her telephone French?

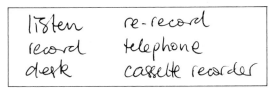

b) Now listen. Did you guess what her strategy was?

c) Could you use this strategy? Why or why not?

### 3 Choose a new strategy

We suggest you experiment with new strategies for practising your speaking in order to find the one(s) you prefer.

---

■ ■ ■ ■ ■ □

## Step 6 Do you need to build up your confidence?

### 1 Thinking-time techniques

a) Read what Dominique says.

*At business meetings sometimes I get asked tricky questions. Often I need time to think about my answer and the English I should use – and there's a big silence. I feel very uncomfortable.*

Dominique, France

Have you ever been in a situation like Dominique's? What did you do?

It's not always easy to speak spontaneously in a foreign language when you're in a tricky situation. This may be because you are nervous about speaking or because you feel you need more time to find the words you need. You can help yourself to sound fluent and in control if you build up your confidence by learning how to use techniques which give you time to think.

⟫→

b) Listen to the cassette for a demonstration of somebody answering a difficult question. Barbara used the following to give herself time to think:
   - repetition of original question
   - 'Ah, yes, now . . .'
   - 'Well, actually . . .'
   - 'That's a very interesting question . . .'
   - '. . . and it's one I've been thinking about for some time . . .'
   - 'You see . . .'
   - 'It's like this . . .'
   - 'How shall I put it? . . .'
   - 'Well, as far as I can see . . .'
   - 'To my mind . . .'

   Can you think of other phrases she could have used? Make a note of them.
   (Other useful techniques can be found in *2.1 Extending vocabulary* Step 6.)

c) Look at the list in (b) and any other items you have added. Choose a few different phrases that you think would be useful for you personally and which you feel happy about using. Practise saying these until you feel confident you can remember them and use them when you need time.

### Activity: Just a Minute!

You can practise the techniques you have just learned by playing *Just a Minute!*
   You will be asked to speak for exactly one minute without stopping on a topic given to you. If it is an easy topic, you probably won't need to use many 'Thinking-time' techniques, but if it is a topic you don't know much about, you will have an ideal opportunity to practise the techniques you have just learned. Only use them if you need them. When you know how to play, you could practise by yourself. You might like to record yourself doing it.
   Listen to Chen and Paz playing the game.

## 2   Suggestions

- Prepare yourself for difficult situations by rehearsing.
- Don't be afraid of making mistakes. Most of the time when you are speaking, it doesn't matter if your English is not always correct.
- In real-life situations, try to avoid using words or phrases that you know are a big problem for you. Try practising them in private until you feel more confident.

■ ■ ■ ■ ■ ■

# Step 7   How do you organise your speaking practice?

Here are some ways of organising your speaking practice.

1. Organise a regular time to practise your speaking.

2. Use a dictionary to help you with pronunciation and stress.

3. Find a cassette 'pen-friend'.*

4. Find out where you can talk to other speakers of English.

5. Have blank cassettes available so you can record yourself.

6. Find materials like poetry and plays that you can read aloud to practise your pronunciation, stress and rhythm.

7. Practise as much as possible.

*A friend you will correspond with by cassette instead of by letter.

## 2.5 Reading

■ □ □ □ □ □ □

### Step 1 How do you feel about reading English?

1. Look at what these learners think about reading English.

*I only read English because I have to. At work I need to read technical manuals and instructions. That's enough for me!*

Roger, France

*I usually give up after a few minutes. It's so slow and boring – always looking up words in my dictionary. I don't enjoy it at all.*

Susanne, W. Germany

*I've always enjoyed reading –
it's one of my hobbies. I often
read books in other languages
too. I like reading detective
stories in English, for example,
and I'm sure I've improved my
English a lot.*

Gilbert, France

2. How do *you* feel about reading English?

3. Find out what other people in your group feel.

■ ■ □ □ □ □ □

## Step 2   What do you know about reading English?

### 1   Reading speed

a) Look at what Stan says about reading.

*It always takes me a long time
to read anything in English –
and it's such hard work.*

Stan, Poland

Do you have problems like Stan's when you read in English?

b) Many people are slow readers in a foreign language because they are so
anxious that they will miss something that they stop and try to understand
every word. Other people are slow readers because they say the words as
they read – either aloud or silently in their minds. What do you do when
you read in your *own* language?                                    ⟫→

81

c) A good reader does not stop and look at every word, but reads several words at a time, in chunks. How many words do you think you can read in the sentence below without moving your eyes?

**A good reader does not stop and look at every word.**

It has been demonstrated that most people can read the first four words of the sentence above without moving their eyes.

d) What are the advantages of reading in chunks? Read the following text to find out.

When reading, instead of moving in smooth lines, the eyes move in a series of stops and quick jumps. See the diagram below:

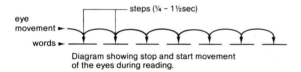

Diagram showing stop and start movement of the eyes during reading.

These jumps are very quick and the stops take from a quarter to one and a half seconds. People who normally read one word at a time – and who skip back over words and letters – are forced into reading speeds which are often well below 100 words per minute. This means that they will not be able to understand much of what they read nor be able to read much. See the diagram below:

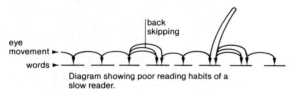

Diagram showing poor reading habits of a slow reader.

This problem can be solved in several ways:
– by reducing back-skipping.
  90% of back-skipping is done only because the reader is anxious and it is unnecessary for understanding.

– by reducing the time for each stop.
  Readers need not fear this because the eye can register as many as five words in one hundredth of a second.
– by reading as many as three to five words at a time. See the diagram below:

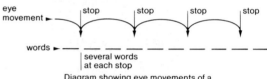

Diagram showing eye movements of a better and more efficient reader.

Slower readers have to do more mental work than faster readers because they have to add the meaning of each word to the meaning of each following word. Faster readers are more efficient because they have to make fewer additions. Another advantage for faster readers is that their eyes will be doing less physical work on each page. Instead of stopping perhaps 500 times per page like slower readers, they will only stop about 100 times per page, which is less tiring for the eye muscles.

Yet another advantage is that the rhythm and flow of fast readers will carry them comfortably through the meaning. Because of all the stopping and starting, slow readers are far more likely to become bored, to lose concentration, to mentally drift away and to lose the meaning of what they are reading.

Adapted from (and for more information in this area read) *Use Your Head* by Tony Buzan

## 2  Reading strategies

A good reader varies his or her reading strategy according to *why* he or she is reading. Having a reason for reading helps you to focus on what you need or want to understand.

When might you use the following strategies?

a) *Skimming:* reading a text quickly just to understand the main ideas.
b) *Scanning:* having a specific point in mind and looking for it quickly in a text.
c) *Reading for detail:* reading a whole text very carefully for specific information.

Can you think of a situation where you really need to understand every word of what you are reading? Give an example if you can.

### Activity: Reading a menu

What strategy would you use to read this menu? Why?

A good reader uses the layout of a text to help him or her understand it. What features of layout helped you to read the menu?

■ ■ ■ □ □ □ □

# Step 3   How well are you doing?

If you are doing a Step 3 for the first time, read the Introduction on page 30 in *2.1 Extending vocabulary*.

### 1   Points to assess

Before you can assess your reading comprehension, it is helpful to think about some of the factors that may help you to understand or prevent you from understanding what you read. You could ask yourself questions, for example:

a) *speed:* Did I read too slowly?
b) *strategy:* Did I use the appropriate reading strategy?
c) *text:* Were there too many words I didn't know?
       Was the grammar too difficult for me?
       Did I know enough about the topic?
       Was the text boring?
       Was the text too long?

When you are assessing your reading comprehension, it is a good idea to concentrate on only one or two of these factors at a time.

### 2   Test yourself in a practice activity

Read what Erik says about testing himself.

*I test my speed and my comprehension like this: I find a short newspaper article and read it once quickly to get the main ideas. Then I cover it up and try to write a brief summary of the main points – sometimes in English, but usually in my own language. Then I compare my summary with the article to see how much I've got. I time myself reading and keep a record of my results.*

Erik, Iceland

 Do you know of any good ways of testing yourself?

### 3   Assess your performance in a real-life situation

Read what Sofia says about assessing herself.

*Following the instructions from the* User Guide *for my new home computer was a real test! If my computer didn't do what I wanted it to do then I knew that I hadn't understood the instructions properly – and so it was back to the* User Guide *again to do some more reading.*

Sofia, Italy

Think of a real-life situation you have been in recently where you needed to read English. Did you have any problems? What were they?

### 4  Examples

This is how Erik and Sofia assessed their reading.

Name: *Erik*

| Date | Activity/Situation | Points to assess | Assessment |
|------|---------------------|------------------|------------|
| *6.1.88* | *Reading newspaper article on sport* | *Speed*<br>*Understanding of main ideas (skimming)* | *2 mins. 50 secs.*<br>*60% of main ideas!*<br>*Speed! Still trying to read every word!* |

Name: *Sofia*

| Date | Activity/Situation | Points to assess | Assessment |
|------|---------------------|------------------|------------|
| *9.4.88* | *Reading User Guide for my home computer* | *Reading for detail* | *Not very good.*<br>*Must learn some more computer vocabulary before I try again.*<br>*Must find out more about how computers work in general.* |

You will find a blank self-assessment chart on page 114 in the Appendix. You could use a copy of this to do your own self-assessment.

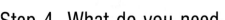

## Step 4   What do you need to do next?

If you are doing a Step 4 for the first time, read the Introduction on page 32 of *2.1 Extending vocabulary.*

**Examples**

Here are examples of how Erik and Sofia set themselves short-term aims.

Name: *Erik*

| What? | How? | When? | How long? | Done |
|-------|------|-------|-----------|------|
| *Improve reading speed* | *Read words in chunks. Read articles as fast as possible: <u>time myself</u>.* | *10.1.88* | *30 mins.* | ✓ |

Name: *Sofia*

| What? | How? | When? | How long? | Done |
|-------|------|-------|-----------|------|
| *Improve comprehension of computer User Guide* | *Learn more computer vocabulary.* | *10.4.88* | *10 mins.* | ✓ |
| | *Read computer manual in Italian.* | *11.4.88* | *1½ hours* | ✓ |

You will find a blank chart which you can copy for your own use on page 115 in the Appendix.

■ ■ ■ ■ ■ □ □

# Step 5 How do you prefer to practise your reading?

### 1 Personal strategies

Read about the strategies used by these learners to practise their reading.

*I choose things to read in English that I would read in my own language. I try to use the same strategy for reading the English as I would for reading the same sort of text in Spanish.*

Sara, Chile

*In the self-access centre I use texts with comprehension questions. I always read the questions before I read the text so that I know what I'm looking for.*

Yuen, Hong Kong

*Once a week I try to go to the British Council library in Tunis. I look through the newspapers and try to find two or three interesting articles to read. I find* The Times *and* The Financial Times *not too difficult to read.*

Borhene, Tunisia

 How do *you* prefer to practise your reading? Can you think of any other ways?

## 2 Suggestions

a) Always be clear about your reason for reading. This will help you select your strategy.

b) It is usually easier to read what is personally interesting for you.

c) Prepare yourself for reading by, for example:
 – finding out about the topic before you start
 – looking at the layout

d) Don't choose anything too difficult! Skim the first page of a novel or reader, for example. If there are more than six key words you don't know and can't guess on the page, you will probably find the book hard work.

e) Read a lot! It helps you to pick up new language.

## 3 Choose a new strategy

We suggest you experiment with new strategies for practising your reading in order to find the one(s) you prefer.

■ ■ ■ ■ ■ □

# Step 6 Do you need to build up your confidence?

## 1 Predicting

When you are reading something in your own language, you can usually predict what comes next. You can try this by taking a sheet of paper and using it to cover the text. Uncover one line at a time and try to guess the next line *before* you uncover it.

There are many things which can help you to predict while you read, for example:
– how much language you already know
– how much you know about the topic
– layout
– grammar
– punctuation
– connectors (and, but, although, however, etc.)
– sequencers (firstly, secondly, next, then, finally, etc.)

*Activity: Completing sentences*

Can you finish these sentences?

a)

> There was some lovely fruit at the market on Thursday: strawberries,

b)

**TWO-DAY FORECASTS**

HOT and sunny in many places, but

c)

# Surgeon on Call

by JANET FERGUSON

### THE STORY SO FAR

Life as staff nurse on an orthopaedic ward in a busy teaching hospital in East Anglia was all CHARIS LANFIELD hoped it would be. Her off-duty hours, too, were happy. She lived with her estate agent father CEDRIC, and their red setter in a comfortable house just outside town and spent a lot of her free time with her fiancé, NEIL, a chartered surveyor in her father's office. But everything was about to change. One day, out shopping, Charis had an argument with a stranger over the ownership of a necklace. Back at the hospital she discovered that GUY MORLAND, the newly-appointed senior registrar on her ward, was none other than her argumentative acquaintance a few hours earlier!

It wasn't long before Charis realised Morland really cared about his patients and, though she didn't like him as a man, she

*Woman's Weekly* 26th July 1986

 Compare your ideas with the rest of the class. What things helped you to guess?

## 2 Guessing unknown words

Good readers try to *guess* the meanings of words they don't know – or simply ignore them if they don't look important for understanding the text. Good readers depend more on themselves than on dictionaries.

There are many clues that can help you guess the meaning of an unknown word. Here are some examples.

*What the word looks like:*
– Has it got a prefix?
  e.g. un-, mis-, dis-, re-, pre-, pro-, etc.
– Has it got a suffix?
  e.g. -ly, -ive, -ment, -able, -ible, etc.
– Is it a compound word?
  e.g. swordfish, steamroller, dipstick, etc.
– Does it look like another word in your own or another language?

*The context:*
e.g. the topic of the text
   the topic of the sentence
   the position of the word in the sentence

### Activity: Guessing out of context

What do you think the following words mean?

| malodorous | unflagging |
| underlay | wobbly |

Which of the above clues helped you?

### Activity: Guessing in context

Look at the above words again in context. What do you think they mean now?

a) The farmer advised me to hold my nose as the pigsty was extremely *malodorous*.
b) The *unflagging* workers picked grapes from sunrise to sunset without a break, and still had enough energy to enjoy the evening festivities.
c) Fred's neighbours downstairs kept complaining about the noise so he bought some *underlay* to put under his carpet.
d) The chair was unsafe to sit on because two of its legs were *wobbly*.

Which activity did you find the most useful for guessing words?

### Activity: Discover the useful tip

Some words in the following text have been replaced by nonsense words. What do you think the original words could have been? For example, in the following sentence:

'I'm *bloppy*; I must eat something soon.';

'bloppy' could mean 'starving', 'famished' or 'hungry'.

The best way to learn new words and their meanings is by (1) *noobling*. By constantly meeting a word in its (2) *scrunge*, you will gradually acquire a group of ideas about the word's over-all meaning. This is a much better way of (3) *squifferising* the meaning of words than referring to your (4) *liag* each time you feel (5) *boofed*.

(1) ...................................................................................................

(2) ...................................................................................................

(3) ...................................................................................................

(4) ...................................................................................................

(5) ...................................................................................................

Adapted from *Panorama* by Ray Williams

■ ■ ■ ■ ■ ■ ■

# Step 7 How do you organise your reading practice?

Here are some suggestions to help you organise your reading practice.

1. Organise a regular time for reading.

2. Collect things to read which interest you personally. Keep a scrapbook of cartoons, recipes, etc. Create your own library of books, articles, etc.

3. Get a pen-friend.

4. Form a reading club with friends so you can exchange books and magazines, etc.

5. Take out a subscription to or place a regular order for an English language magazine or newspaper.

# 2.6 Writing

---
■ □ □ □ □ □
---

## Step 1 How do you feel about writing English?

1. Didier, Bernhard and Tanim have different attitudes towards writing English.

Didier, France

*If I have a choice between writing or using the telephone, I always write. It's safer! I've got time to think about what I want to say.*

*Most of the writing I do in English is just to help me learn – spelling, phrases etc. I remember new things better if I write them.*

Bernhard, W. Germany

*I enjoy Writing English*
*I like the Shape of the letters*

Tanim, Afghanistan

 2. How do *you* feel about writing English?

 3. Find out what other people in your group feel.

■ ■ ☐ ☐ ☐ ☐

# Step 2  What do you know about writing English?

### 1  What do people write?

People generally write *either* to communicate something to other people (the writing is meant to be read by others) *or* for their own personal use (the writing is not usually meant to be read by others).

The diagram which follows shows some different types of writing.

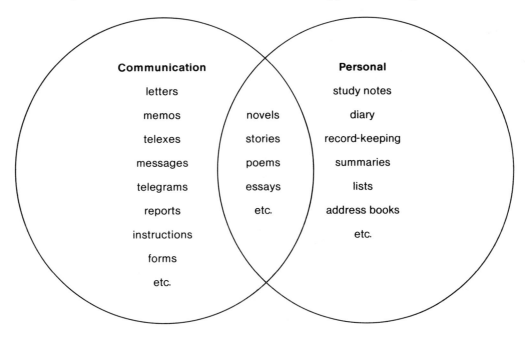

**Communication**

letters

memos

telexes

messages

telegrams

reports

instructions

forms

etc.

novels

stories

poems

essays

etc.

**Personal**

study notes

diary

record-keeping

summaries

lists

address books

etc.

Can you think of other types of writing to add to the diagram?

### 2  Characteristics of written texts

Written English differs from spoken English in a number of ways (see *2.4 Speaking* Step 2). In addition, different types of written texts have their own characteristics which you need to know about if you want to be able to write successfully.

*Activity: Comparing written texts*

a) If possible, bring to class an example of writing by a native speaker of English. Try to bring the type of writing you need or want to be able to do, for example:
    a business letter
    a telex
    a poem

b) Work with another class member who has brought in a different type of

written text. Compare your examples and make a note of the specific characteristics that make them different from each other, for example:
  layout
  style of language
  length
  organisation of ideas, etc.

 c) Compare your findings with the rest of the class and make notes under the following headings:

  *Type of written text*
  *Specific characteristics*

### 3   What are the features of a well-written text?

If you are writing a text for someone else to read, it is important to keep your reader constantly in mind so that you write in a way that he or she will understand.

 What do you think are the features of a well-written text? Make a list.

*Activity: Detective work*

a) Read letter A on page 95, which was written by a non-native speaker, and compare it with version B on page 96, where it has been rewritten by a native speaker. What changes has the native speaker made and how have they improved the letter?

b) Can you add any more items to your list of the features of a well-written text?

 c) Which ones do you think are the most important? Why?

This activity is known as 'reformulation'. Reformulation is when a native speaker rewrites something you have written in order to improve it, but does not change your original meaning. This technique is useful for improving your writing because it makes you think about style and organisation as well as your grammar, vocabulary and spelling, etc.

  You could ask a native or a good speaker of English to reformulate some of your writing. Show him or her the examples in the activity if necessary.

Letter A

September 8, 1988

7, Balsahan, Binakayan
Kawit, Cavita
Philippines

Application Letter

To the Hotel Management

TO WHOM IT MAY CONCERN:

Dear Sir:

As far as I'm concern I'm very glad to inform you that I'm very much interested in joining your prestigeous and reknown Five Star Hotel in the whole world. And now I'm very much committed about myself, that I was oblige to send you some farther information regarding about my self-being.

As you would'nt know, I'm previously employed too at the Philippine Grand Five Star Hotel which is a member of a famous international Hotels Chain around the world. Being employed in the hotel; I might say that it does have me a knowledge when it comes to hotel experience job.

But before this hotel experience I have, I've also attended a seminar which deal for a Tourism & Hotel Management Course. Which is given by Universal Institute of Tourism & Hotel Administration a few years ago on November 1979.

Meanwhile on this application letter of mine it included too my Personal Data together with all my work experience that happens to me. And now for this matter, I may say that you already have some further information regarding my personality.

For this time in order that I may accomplished my goal, it's your turn now to judge me with your most convenient conclusion so that you may arrived to the right answers whether if I'm qualified or not.

Hopefully; due to a great perseverance of the people here in applying for a job abroad, and I was convince to choose the hotels as a decent work. Besides I already have a hotel work experience.

I hope you will extend to me your kind consideration on this matter. And I'll do appreciate it a lot. Please farther acknowledge my application.

Thanks and my warmest regards.

Very truly yours,

Letter B

7, Balsahan, Binakayan,
Kawit, Cavita,
Philippines

8th September, 1988

Dear Sir or Madam,

I would very much like to apply for a post in your hotel.

As I have previously been employed by the Philippine Grand Hotel, a member of a well-known international hotel chain, you will already have my personal data and details regarding my past working experience.  While working there, I was able to gain a great deal of knowledge and experience of the hotel industry.  However, I am including some further information with this letter in support of my application.

In November 1979 I followed a course on 'Tourism and Hotel Management' at the Universal Institute of Tourism and Hotel Administration.  Furthermore, I have found hotel work very satisfying and rewarding and am very committed to this type of work.

If you consider me to be a suitable candidate for a post in your hotel, I would welcome the opportunity to work abroad in order to expand my hotel work experience.

I hope you will consider my application favourably and I look forward to hearing from you.

Yours faithfully

■ ■ ■ □ □ □ □

# Step 3  How well are you doing?

If you are doing a Step 3 for the first time, read the Introduction on page 30 in *2.1 Extending vocabulary*.

## 1  Points to assess

Before you can assess your writing, you need to be clear about what exactly you want to assess. Look back at the list of features of a well-written text that you made in Step 2(3).

The points you choose to assess and how detailed your assessment is will depend on whether you are writing something for somebody else to read or for your own personal use, as well as on the type of text you are writing. For example, if you are writing a job application you will aim to produce a piece of writing which is as good and as correct as possible. This may mean you write several drafts and you will probably be very detailed and critical in your self-assessment. If, however, you are taking notes from a lecture in English, your points for self-assessment will be limited to 'Can I understand my notes?' Later, when you are writing your essay from these notes, you may assess yourself on many more points because your writing will be read by someone else.

*Invent your own marking scheme*

Once you have selected your points to assess, it is helpful to ask yourself questions, such as:
   'How clearly were my ideas presented and linked?'
   'How correct was my spelling?'

To answer these questions you need to be able to analyse your own writing. You could use symbols, such as the ones suggested here, to indicate what kinds of mistakes you have made. You can then see very clearly what your problems are.

   tense form incorrect Ⓣ

   spelling incorrect Ⓢⓟ

   linking word missing Ⓧ

What other kinds of mistakes might you find? What symbols could you use to indicate them?

*Activity: Marking an essay*

Look at Sabine's essay on page 98 and use your symbols to indicate her mistakes. Can you correct them?
   What do you think Sabine needs to improve most?

⟫→

97

## The average german family

The average german family lives in a flat or in a maisonnette with a garden.

I live in a maisonnette with my parents and my grandmother but I have my own dwelling.

Our house have three floors and a basement. We have three living-rooms, three kitchen and three bathrooms.

I work in a bank for 40 hours a week.

I starts at 7 in the morning and finishes at 15.45 in the evening. I go to work by bus and tube, which I takes 30 minutes.

At the evening sometimes I watching television or I go with my friends in a disco or in a pub. My hobbys are squash, to dance and ski.

Saline,

## 2   Test yourself in a practice activity

Read Javier's suggestion for testing himself.

*I take a business letter, for example, and read it and make notes on the content. Then I try to reconstruct the letter from my notes. I compare my version with the original letter to see how well I've done.*

Javier, Argentina

 Do you know of any other good ways of testing yourself?

### 3   Assess your performance in a real-life situation

Read what Mazharuddin says about assessing himself.

*I'm studying medicine in London and I do a lot of practice examinations. I always give myself plenty of time to read everything I've written very carefully. I check spelling, grammar and punctuation.*

Mazharuddin, India

 Think of a real-life situation you have been in recently where you needed to write English. How well do you think you wrote?

### 4   Examples

This is how Javier and Mazharuddin assessed themselves.

Name: *Javier*

| Date | Activity/Situation | Points to assess | Assessment |
|------|--------------------|------------------|------------|
| *14.8.88* | *Reconstructing a business letter* | *Vocabulary* *Spelling* *Grammar* *Punctuation* | *OK* *Not satisfied* *OK: gerunds* *No problem* |

Name: *Mazharuddin*

| Date | Activity/Situation | Points to assess | Assessment |
|------|--------------------|------------------|------------|
| *14.8.88* | *Practice examinations (2nd MBBS Anatomy paper 1985)* | *Organisation of ideas* *Spelling* *Grammar* *Punctuation* | *Not logical Use of connectors and sequencers* *OK* *OK, but . . . 2nd conditionals (again!)* *OK* |

You will find a blank self-assessment chart on page 114 in the Appendix. You could use a copy of this to do your own self-assessment.

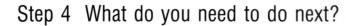

## Step 4   What do you need to do next?

If you are doing a Step 4 for the first time, read the Introduction on page 32 in *2.1 Extending vocabulary*.

### Examples

Here are examples of how Javier and Mazharuddin set themselves short-term aims.

Name: *Javier*

| What? | How? | When? | How long? | Done |
|---|---|---|---|---|
| *Improve spelling* | *Copy out three times and test myself.* | *15.8.88* | *10 mins.* | ✓ |
| *Use of gerunds* | *Look for more examples in my file of business letters and write them in my grammar Pattern Bank.* | | *25 mins.* | ✓ |

Name: *Mazharuddin*

| What? | How? | When? | How long? | Done |
|---|---|---|---|---|
| *Improve use of:*<br>*— connectors*<br>*— sequencers* | *Write notes first and organise them. Add connectors and sequencers. Then write out in full.* | *15.8.88* | *1 hour* | ✓ |

You will find a blank chart which you can copy for your own use on page 115 in the Appendix.

■ ■ ■ ■ □ □

# Step 5 How do you prefer to practise your writing?

### 1 Personal strategies

Read about the strategies used by these learners to practise their writing.

I belong to Amnesty International and I use their guidelines for writing letters to the "Prisoners of the Month" for practising writing. It's a good way to learn and I feel good about it, too.

Ernst, W. Germany

I've got pen-friends around the world who I write to regularly.

Maria Jesus, Peru

While I'm in this country, I try to keep a personal diary in English.

Luang, Singapore

Martine, Luxembourg

I've really started to enjoy English now I've got a word processor at home. I can store different types of writing. Practising writing in English isn't such hard work and I can correct myself easily.

How do *you* prefer to practise your writing? Can you think of any other ways?

## 2  Time to experiment

*Writing drafts*

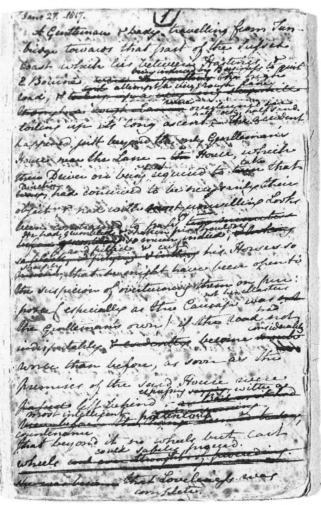Train yourself to think in English. It is usually not a good idea to compose what you want to say in your own language first and then try to translate it. Why not?

Train yourself to write directly in English as much as possible. If you do this, you will be activating the English you already know and will need to spend less time using dictionaries.

One way of training yourself to do this is by writing drafts. A draft is a preparation for the final version of your writing. You may write several drafts before you are satisfied.

Below you can see an example of a draft for *Sanditon* (1817) which was written by the novelist Jane Austen (1775–1817).

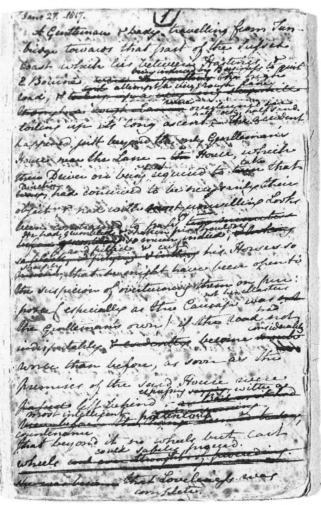

Try not to stop at all to check in dictionaries while you are writing. You can do this when you have finished.

*Activity: Class guide*

You have been asked to produce a brief guide for new students joining your class next term.

a) Decide what information you think a new student would want to know.

b) Decide how you are going to present it.

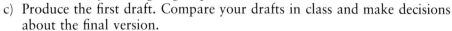 c) Produce the first draft. Compare your drafts in class and make decisions about the final version.

*Activity: Create a magazine*

As a project, you could either create your own magazine or work together with other students to create a class magazine containing articles, puzzles, letters, reviews, poems, jokes, recipes, etc.

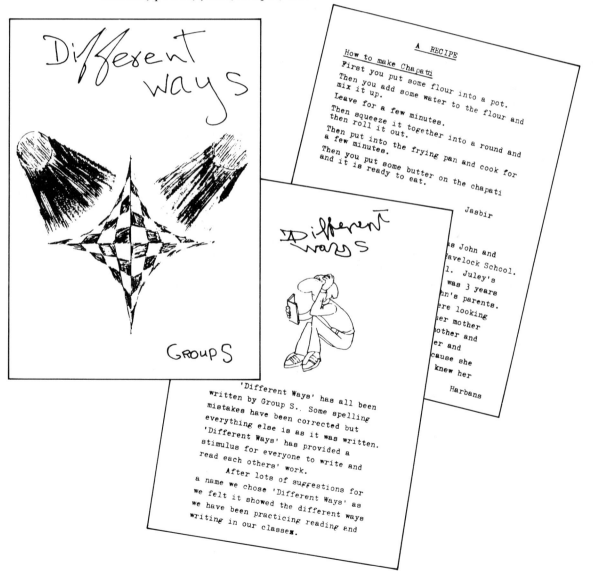

## 3 Suggestions

*Model Banks*

- Collect examples of the types of writing you need/want to do.
- Keep them in a file or a scrapbook for easy reference.
- If possible, make copies of your 'Models' for other people in your class who may want to collect them.

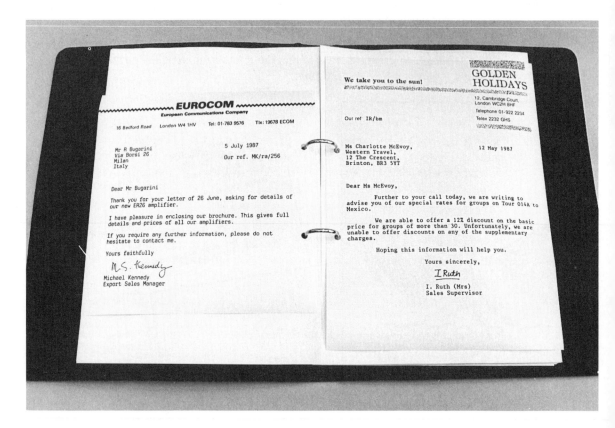

*Memorise*

Learn useful expressions that you need to use regularly in your writing. Here are some examples:

> Thank you for your letter of 9th June.
> I'm looking forward to hearing from you soon.
> Yours sincerely,
> Yours faithfully,

## 4 Choose a new strategy

We suggest you experiment with new strategies for practising your writing in order to find the one(s) you prefer.

■ ■ ■ ■ ■ □

# Step 6  Do you need to build up your confidence?

### Writing spontaneously

When you are writing, you usually have time to think about what you want to say, to use aids such as dictionaries and grammar books, or to ask for help. However, you can sometimes become too dependent on these aids. What are some of the disadvantages of this?

There are ways you can train yourself to become more confident and independent, for example, by giving yourself practice in writing drafts (see Step 5). You could also try the following activities; they will help you to think in English and to write spontaneously without worrying about making mistakes.

*Activity: Dictation*

Your teacher will dictate part of a text to you and then ask you to continue writing the text on your own. You should try to develop the topic further and use the same style. When you have finished, read your text to the class.

*Activity: Timed writing*

a) *Five minutes:* Your teacher will give you a topic to write about for five minutes. Write as much as you can. Read your text to the other learners in your group.

b) *Two minutes:* Your teacher will give you a topic and ask you to write as much as possible in two minutes. The student who has written the longest text is the winner. Your text should make sense!

Here are some examples of timed writing (2 minutes) on 'My Country'.

The place I Come from People walk up
Site down. legs up and hands down, if you
ask me why, I don't Know.
Over main meal are rise, cheicken, Beef.
veg tiable.
When we inv, te friends or relative, we do
a very tasty and chilishes food. not like Some
wt were else. one important thing is they

Kadir, Iraq

≫→

105

*The weather in my country is good because it is in Tropical. Food is a bit spicey. We can grow everything easily. It is the rich land.*

Vanna, Cambodia

*My name is Sritorn Haggard I come from Thailand I'm 26 years old. I really enjoy in my country. We have the king and Queen. We have moan 3000 temple. I like the*

Sritorn, Thailand

■ ■ ■ ■ ■ ■

## Step 7  How do you organise your writing practice?

Here are some suggestions for organising your writing practice.

1.  Organise a regular time for practising writing.

2.  Get a pen-friend.

3.  Keep a Model Bank (see Step 5).

4.  Keep copies of everything you write in English (letters etc.) to use as reference.

5.  Copy texts in English. If possible, learn to type or use a word processor.

# Appendix

Note: The charts in this appendix may be photocopied for use by learners.

**Needs analysis chart (1.3)**

| Situations | Skills | | | | | |
|---|---|---|---|---|---|---|
| | Vocabulary (✓) | Grammar (✓) | Listening (✓) | Speaking (✓) | Reading (✓) | Writing (✓) |
| | | | | | | |
| | | | | | | |
| | | | | | | |
| | | | | | | |
| | | | | | | |
| | | | | | | |

## Self-assessment scale (1.3)

| Extending vocabulary | Dealing with grammar | Listening | Speaking | Reading | Writing |
|---|---|---|---|---|---|
| 1 | 1 | 1 | 1 | 1 | 1 |
| 2 | 2 | 2 | 2 | 2 | 2 |
| 3 | 3 | 3 | 3 | 3 | 3 |
| 4 | 4 | 4 | 4 | 4 | 4 |
| 5 | 5 | 5 | 5 | 5 | 5 |

## Record of priorities (1.3)

| Skill | Priority rating |
|---|---|
| Extending vocabulary | |
| Dealing with grammar | |
| Listening | |
| Speaking | |
| Reading | |
| Writing | |

**Dictionary chart (1.4)**

| Title | Date published | Number of headwords | Bilingual/ Monolingual | Portable? | Examples of how words are used? |
|-------|----------------|---------------------|------------------------|-----------|---------------------------------|
|       |                |                     |                        |           |                                 |

**Grammar book chart (1.4)**

| Title | Date published | Bilingual/ Monolingual | Clear index? | Easy to understand? | Examples in context? | Exercises? | Answers to exercises? |
|---|---|---|---|---|---|---|---|
|  |  |  |  |  |  |  |  |

*Appendix*

## Motivation graph (1.5)

Name:                                                    Date:

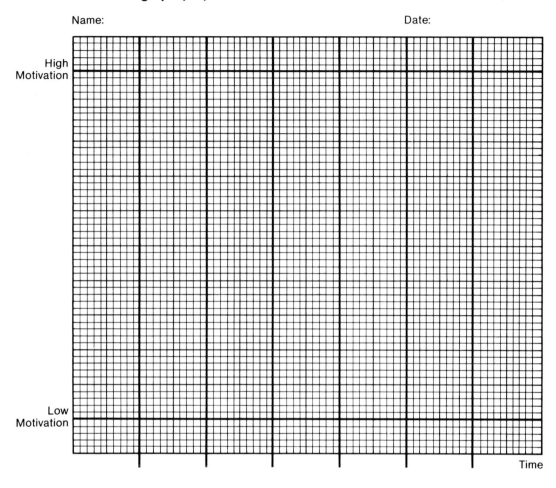

| Day | Comments |
|-----|----------|
|     |          |

**Self-assessment chart (Step 3)**

| Date | Activity/Situation | Points to assess | Assessment |
|------|--------------------|------------------|------------|
|      |                    |                  |            |

**Short-term aims chart (Step 4)**

| What? | How? | When? | How long? | Done |
|---|---|---|---|---|
| | | | | |

**1 Useful addresses** – these are in Britain unless otherwise stated

*Radio*

*London Calling* – the programme journal of the BBC World Service. This contains a guide to the current recommended transmission times and frequencies for your area. For a free copy and subscription form write to:

**London Calling**
PO Box 76
Bush House
Strand
London WC2B 4PH

*BBC English* – a bi-monthly magazine based on the BBC's *English by Radio* broadcasts. For subscription rates and further information write to one of the following offices.

**UK and the rest of the world**
World of Information
21 Gold Street
Saffron Walden
Essex CB10 1EJ

**West Germany**
Buchhandlung Stäheli & Co
Am Marktplatz 20
D-7208 Spaichingen/Württ

**N. America**
World of Information
PO Box C-430
Birmingham
AL 35283-0430
USA

**France**
W. H. Smith & Son SA
17 rue Lamandé
75017 Paris

*Organisations*

For information on short and summer courses in English as a foreign language and specialised English write to:

**English Teaching Information Centre**
Central Information Service
The British Council
10 Spring Gardens
London SW1A 2BN

*ARELS-FELCO* – a professional association of private English language schools and organisations recognised as efficient by the British Council. They produce a guide for foreign students called *Learn English in Britain with ARELS-FELCO*.
Write to:

**ARELS-FELCO**
2 Pontypool Place
Valentine Place
London SE1 8FQ

**BASCELT** – (British Association of State Colleges in English Language Teaching)
HGS Institute
Central Square
London NW11 7BN

**British Tourist Authority**
Thames Tower
Black's Road
Hammersmith
London W6 9EL

**British Travel Centre**
4 Lower Regent Street
London SW1

*Magazines*

**Viewfinder** – a magazine for students studying for Cambridge First Certificate
ELA
21 High Street
Shrivenham
Oxfordshire

**Mary Glasgow Publications Ltd** – for information about a range of magazines
Avenue House
131–3 Holland Park Avenue
London W11 4UT

*Examining Bodies*

For English Language Testing Service, Cambridge and Royal Society of Arts exams:

**UCLES** (University of Cambridge Local Examinations Syndicate)
1 Hills Road
Cambridge CB1 2EU

For Oxford exams:

**University of Oxford Delegacy of Local Examinations**
Ewert House
Ewert Place
Sommertown
Oxford OX2 7BZ

For ARELS exams:

**The ARELS Examinations Trust**
Ewert House
Ewert Place
Sommertown
Oxford OX2 7BZ

*Appendix*

For further useful addresses and general information about life in Britain see
*Discover Britain* (CUP 1988).

Use the chart below for recording useful addresses in your country, e.g. The
British Council, BTA.

| Address | Useful for |
| --- | --- |
|  |  |